UNDERGROUND
PRIVACY
SECRETS

HOW TO PROTECT YOUR PRIVACY, IDENTITY AND FREEDOM IN AN INCREASINGLY UNFREE WORLD!

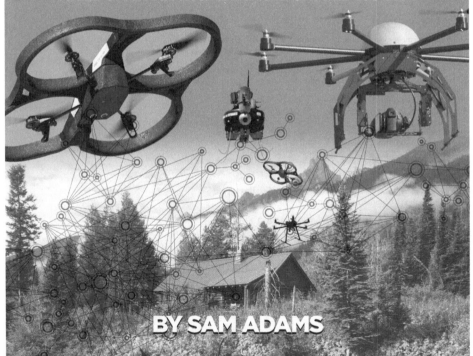

BY SAM ADAMS

Published by:

Shallow Creek
Publishers

An imprint of Heritage Press Publications, LLC
PO Box 561
Collinsville, MS 39325

Cover photos courtesy of:

Nicolas Halftermeyer via Wikimedia Commons (Parrot AR Drone)
Captain Dave Scammell/MOD via Wikimedia Commons (T-Hawk Remote Air System)

http://commons.wikimedia.org/wiki/File:National_Security_Agency,_2013.jpg
By Trevor Paglen via Wikimedia Commons

http://en.wikipedia.org/wiki/File:Edward_Snowden-2.jpg
By Laura Poitras/Praxis Films via Wikimedia Commons

http://en.wikipedia.org/wiki/File:PRISM_logo_%28PNG%29.png
By Adam Hart-Davis via Wikimedia Commons

http://en.wikipedia.org/wiki/File:NYC_IRS_office_by_Matthew_Bisanz.JPG
By Matthew G. Bisanz via Wikimedia Commons

http://commons.wikimedia.org/wiki/File:Nashville_Tea_Party.jpg
By Kevin Smith via Wikimedia Commons

http://commons.wikimedia.org/wiki/File:RFID_hand_2.jpg
By Amal Graafstra via Wikimedia Commons

http://commons.wikimedia.org/wiki/File:RFID_hand_1.jpg
By Amal Graafstra via Wikimedia Commons

http://commons.wikimedia.org/wiki/File:US_drone_infrared_image.jpg
By USAF drone pilot, Brandon Bryant via Wikimedia Commons

ISBN-10: 1937660265

ISBN-13: 978-1-937660-26-0

DISCLAIMER

Although the author and publisher have made every effort to ensure that the information in this book was correct at press time, the author and the publisher do not assume, and hereby disclaim, any liability to any party for any loss, damage, or disruption caused by errors or omissions, whether such errors or omissions result from negligence, accident, or any other cause.

Information contained in this book is intended as an educational aid only and for general informational purposes only. It is not intended as legal or financial advice, and is not a substitute for the assistance from expert legal or financial guides and their services.

CONTENTS

INTRODUCTION

What is privacy? Merriam-Webster.com defines the word privacy first as:

The state of being alone: the state of being away from other people.

However, it is not the state of being alone or merely being away from other people that raises privacy concerns in this era of American history. You don't always have to be alone in order to attain privacy. The privacy we are concerned about has to do with who you are as a person, the content of your information, and your liberty to preserve the anonymity and confidentiality of them both. This is why Merriam-Webster.com provides us with an additional definition of privacy below, which says:

Freedom from unauthorized intrusion. <one's right to privacy>

It is this freedom from unauthorized intrusion that has inspired the writing of this book. These days, unauthorized intrusion seems to be committed on an hourly basis, as cases of identity theft continue to happen more and more often. Identity theft happens when a criminal uses the name and information of a victim in order to steal from him or her, impersonate the victim for financial gain, or use his or her information to commit a crime in the victim's name. As you will see later in this book, the statistics on identity theft appear to show a steady increase in frequency, sophistication, and organization of this type of crime.

However, identity theft is not the only kind of privacy invasion that we must be concerned about. In fact, our transactions, online searches, locations, and even our eating habits are being documented, catalogued, and stored for marketing purposes. Major corporations are beginning to understand the value of information that is unknowingly (and often unwillingly) being provided by their own customers. At this point, the corporations who utilize this data mining are doing so for profit. I don't believe that their intent is malicious. However, I'm completely convinced that they are middlemen in a grander scheme.

This is why we will spend a large portion of this book concentrating on the government's attempt to spy upon the American people. While corporations may invasively spy upon us, their ability to use that information for coercion is very limited. However, the government has the capability of coercion of the worst kind: the ability to kill, take away freedom, and confiscate property.

Thus, when the U.S. government is caught spying (as we discovered in the summer of 2013), it is time to pay attention. In addition, it is important to understand the scope of their spying programs.

You may think that because there are just so many people out there to watch that the government isn't watching *you*. Besides, *you aren't a terrorist!* There's no reason for them to go through all that trouble, right?

In the coming chapters, you may discover that this assumption may not be very accurate. Indeed, there are a lot of people to watch, but the government is quickly accumulating the infrastructure to do so effectively.

Philosophically speaking, you may simply be someone who is generally a good person and law-abiding citizen. You may be a person who feels, "I have nothing to hide, because I've done nothing wrong. I don't care if they can watch me." This is a valid point, but only if the facts don't change, good laws are enforced, and the Constitution is still followed. However, we are seeing a slow transition from the rule of law to anarchical tyranny, and it's a transition that appears to be picking up the pace.

The important part to remember is the fact that regimes can change overnight, and a government's laws can be altered within hours. The liberty-protecting laws that we enjoy today may no longer be in place tomorrow; however, the ability to track you will not go away any time soon. Infrastructure does not merely disappear. In fact, a tyrant would throw the surveillance system into high gear.

This is why I emphasize the understanding that you should not trust in people, personalities, or governments. Instead, it's important to trust in sturdy laws, which are quickly and strongly enforced. The most important laws have little to do with keeping the citizenry in check, but rather with keeping the government in check.

Laws are impersonal and impartial. Laws cannot change except through the same types of processes that enacted them in the first place. No one is above the law, and that includes members of the government. This is why we do not follow politicians in our constitutional republic—we follow laws.

Understanding this point, I take much of the inspiration for this book from a very familiar classic novel called 1984. It is not a particular group or party that has the propensity to form a tyranny. Rather, it is human nature itself, which is liberty's bitterest enemy:

> *Now I will tell you the answer to my question. It is this. The Party seeks power entirely for its own sake. We are not interested in the good of others; we are interested solely in power, pure power. What pure power means you will understand presently. We are different from the oligarchies of the past in that we know what we are doing. All the others, even those who resembled ourselves, were cowards and hypocrites. The German Nazis and the Russian Communists came very close to us in their methods, but they never had the courage to recognize their own motives. They pretended, perhaps they even believed, that they had seized power unwillingly and for a limited time, and that just around the corner there lay a paradise where human beings would be free and equal. We are not like that. We know that no one ever seizes power with the intention of relinquishing it. Power is not a means; it is an end. One does not establish a dictatorship in order to safeguard a revolution; one makes the revolution in order to establish the dictatorship. The object of persecution is persecution. The object of torture is torture. The object of power is power. Now you begin to understand me. – George Orwell, 1984*

The significance of my references to 1984 revolves around the fact that it is the type of world that we dearly want to avoid.

With every perpetration of identity theft, it gives the government even more of an excuse to sweep in to "protect us." With the continued advancement of technology in our lives, it gives corporations another means by which to track us. To paraphrase Benjamin Franklin, every time we sacrifice our freedom for a little security on the bureaucratic altars in Washington D.C., we prove that we deserve neither.

THE SOLUTION?

The solution to these issues is rather simple: rather than looking to someone else for our ability to maintain our privacy, perhaps it is time we look to ourselves.

However, I'm not in favor of starting fires, and I'm not really looking to change minds that are willingly deceived. I'm speaking to people like *you*. I'm trying to reach the good folks who are already interested enough in privacy to pick up this book.

You are the ones I want to reach.

This book is for those who endeavor to be responsible, self-sufficient, and logical. It is for people who are not interested in a fight, but instead are looking to avoid fights by disappearing. Also, I am speaking to folks who follow laws and not those who are law-breakers. I am not speaking to those involved in criminality, but instead to those who wish to keep criminality from entering their lives. I am not speaking to victims; I am not even speaking to survivors. No, I am speaking to those who want to thrive with their dignity intact when the worst trials and tribulations approach.

You will note that in the last chapters of this book, I discuss a plan called "The Invisibility Objective." This plan contains three basic stages to attain adequate privacy protection. In the Invisibility Objective, the first topic of discussion is identity theft. Essentially, I will show you how to beat identity theft using simple steps and methods to make it very difficult to locate you, extract your data, and get away with it if the first two stages fail.

Interestingly enough, many of the most basic principles of the Invisibility Objective can be applied to a wide range of crimes from petty muggings to government crimes against humanity.

The Invisibility Objective will go into detail about the basics on how to disappear during a state of tyranny in America. The information in this book is comprehensive, but I chose to leave the specifics up to you. Because of the rapidly changing world of banking, privacy, and international law, I decided to give information that will remain timeless…so, for the most part, instead of naming certain companies, attorneys, etc., I point you in the general direction so that you can find your own information.

Ultimately, the purpose of the Invisibility Objective is not to enable citizens to commit crimes, but instead to enable citizens to refuse to be *victims* of crimes. Indeed, it does appear to be a fine line between the two, which is why additional research must be done on your part pertaining to the laws of your own municipality.

Also, since I am not legal professional, I am not giving legal advice. Only your attorney can do that. Finding a good attorney who handles these kinds of things is highly recommended if you begin to tackle the Invisibility Objective. Getting into trouble would certainly be self-defeating, so be sure that you access the legal advice you need in order to achieve your privacy objectives.

IT CAN BE DONE

To get the most out of this book, it is important that you take notes, continue researching, and don't treat these pages gently. Use pens, pencils, markers, or whatever will help you learn as much as possible from what I will be discussing in *Underground Privacy Secrets*.

This book is meant to be a guide and even provide you with a ray of hope. I do not want you to get halfway through the book and think that it is impossible to have privacy and protect your identity. Keep in mind that I will paint some dismal and dark scenarios, but I do not put those in this book for the purpose of making you afraid or to feel helpless. I do so in order to give you an accurate view of the problem—and then I provide a workable solution that solves those problems. I mean it when I say the words, "It can be done."

This is essentially the message I am trying to get across. I am not here to preach (although I do discuss philosophy and law to justify my position). Instead, I am here to enable. It is only through your self-empowerment that my objective will be successfully achieved. The Invisibility Objective is interesting in that it really *cannot* be tackled by anyone but you. If you were to entrust someone else with your privacy, then it would be completely self-defeating. Your privacy is in your keeping alone, and to place something so important in someone else's hands would immediately nullify your efforts.

With that said, you should keep in mind that some of these suggestions are by no means free (in terms of money). Many of the suggestions may cost you quite a bit of money and may even consume your life savings. However, where you would hypothetically spend the most is on investments and not on temporary assets. The plan at the very end was crafted with an understanding of the "threat versus resources" balance and set up chronologically so that you aren't making any large purchases unless you've also taken care of the cheaper, essential parts of the plan first.

MOVING FORWARD

And so, without any further delay, let's get into *Underground Privacy Secrets*. I hope that you thoroughly enjoy learning how to protect yourself from threats small and massive, being able to outsmart the most intelligent and ruthless of criminals, and ultimately enjoying the peace of mind you will find when you realize that you and your loved ones will be okay.

It can be done. You can make this happen. Now, sit back, and let's see how to win the war on your privacy.

In Section One, we will discuss the grand scope of how personal privacy is being chipped away in the United States. Identity theft is only a small part of an overarching criminal epidemic that is poised to invade our privacy and destroy our liberty.

SECTION ONE

What Is Happening to Our to Our Privacy Rights?

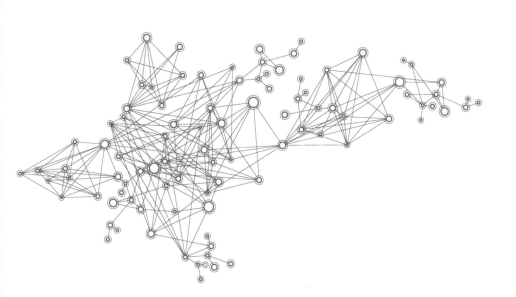

Chapter 1

LIBERTY AND PRIVACY CODIFIED

If you were to scour the U.S. Constitution for the word "privacy," you might come up a bit disappointed. In fact, the Fourth Amendment never actually states that U.S. citizens have the right to privacy. Instead, the Fourth Amendment states,

> *The right of the people to be secure in their persons, houses, papers, and effects, against unreasonable searches and seizures, shall not be violated, and no Warrants shall issue, but upon probable cause, supported by Oath or affirmation, and particularly describing the place to be searched, and the persons or things to be seized.*

During the first days of the great American experiment, the right to privacy was simply an implied aspect of having freedom. In essence, it was the ability to be secure in your assets, and that the government was not allowed to take a peek into your affairs, except through operating from due process of law. No, the government was never allowed to see your papers unless there were very specific and limited powers issued to the magistrate by law. The neck of the state was bound by the Constitution (the law of the land), and the government was on a short leash in terms of how it could enforce its will upon the people.

This was not a new idea, even as far back as 1787 when the Constitution was ratified. In fact, this idea of being secure in your personal property was passed into English law in 1225 A.D. through the Magna Carta. The Magna Carta essentially bound the hands of the king (more specifically, King John of England), and it brought about the understanding that no freeman could be punished by the government, except through law. Indeed, even the government was forced to obey the law, just like everyone else.

Lord Denning described the Magna Carta's power against the power-obsessed, saying that it was,

"[T]he greatest constitutional document of all times—the foundation of the freedom of the individual against the arbitrary authority of the despot."

This understanding of personal liberty is well over 800 years old. Thus, it is no wonder why colonial Americans decided to go to war with England over basic freedoms, which were slowly being chipped away by King George. These days, it is called the Revolutionary War, but it was far from revolutionary. Rather, the Crown engaged in a revolutionary abandonment of basic law-protected liberties, which were already several hundred years old at that point.

The thirteen colonies fought the Crown in a counter-revolution, trying to separate from cancerous eighteenth-century England. This is why the war has historically been known as the War for Independence. In essence, the Crown broke the English common law and the colonies wanted this law back in power.

The understanding that law should protect personal liberty and property is more English than American. Even in 1604 (only 172 years prior to the War for Independence), Sir Edmund Coke stated, "The house of every one is to him as his castle and fortress, as well for his defense against injury and violence as for his repose."

For hundreds of years, the preservation of laws that protect private property has been the cornerstone of our most basic freedoms.

WHAT IS FREEDOM?

When someone says, "It's a free country," or drops a catch phrase like, "Freedom isn't free," what do they even mean? Most popular figureheads have no idea concerning what makes America a free country.

Many call the U.S. a democracy, which could not be further from the truth. In fact, James Madison, our fourth U.S. president, once said,

"Democracy is the most vile form of government...democracies have ever been spectacles of turbulence and contention...incompatible with personal security or the rights of property."

The ability to cast a vote has little to do with what makes a nation free. An unwitting public has voted some of the most despotic regimes into power. Democracy has been a prevalent cause of bloody war, poverty, and especially tyranny. Why? Simply put, it is extremely easy to deceive a population into handing over power and freedom with it. If you don't believe me, simply flip on the news and see for yourself. Even countries like Hussein-controlled Iraq and Chavez-controlled Venezuela were considered democracies.

Also, the German people democratically voted Adolph Hitler into power. (Then again, Hitler did make *Time Magazine's* Man of the Year in 1938, so he must have seemed like a good guy.) The world can thank democracy for the unfortunate butchery of millions in the last century.

So, what makes the U.S. a free country? The answer lies in an understanding about where power originates, flows, and where it ends up.

The most historically traditional view says that power begins with God (whichever higher deity you prefer), and then flows to the sovereignty of the people (general populace), which finally trickles down into the hands of the government (local, state, federal). This system is most consistent with a constitutional republic, which is what the U.S. is (and was back in 1787).

Under a democracy, the power begins with the government and then flows to the people, and then to law with your higher deity somewhere at the bottom. The reason why democracy has such a tendency to develop into tyranny is due to the fact that law and order are based on the whims of mere bureaucrats and politicians, which is then influenced by ever-changing public opinion. Simply put, if you can change the will of the public through a well-oiled media machine, you can control the nation with ease.

In a constitutional republic, it is much harder to take despotic control since there are checks and balances at every turn. Even the U.S. president must answer to the laws in the Constitution. The people have the power to be free because the law makes it so. No one individual (or group) can usurp the power of a broken up and checked government, which derives its power from law that is very difficult to alter.

The foundation of freedom is the law, which everyone must follow. This is why those who are advocates for privacy rights always refer back to the Fourth Amendment of the U.S. Constitution.

WHY THE FOURTH AMENDMENT MATTERS

Understanding that freedom stems from God and the Constitution and not from public opinion (and especially not from politicians and the government), it is easy to understand why the Fourth Amendment is so important for your privacy. Let us go back again and restate the text of the Fourth Amendment:

> *The right of the people to be secure in their persons, houses, papers, and effects, against unreasonable searches and seizures, shall not be violated, and no Warrants shall issue, but upon probable cause, supported by Oath or affirmation, and particularly describing the place to be searched, and the persons or things to be seized.*

The Fourth Amendment makes it unbelievably difficult for the government to take a peek into your personal affairs. Of course, it does not completely strip the government's ability to look into the business of a suspect, but there are stringent laws protecting a U.S. citizen from a peeping-Tom-style government. If the individual truly needs to be investigated, then there should be little problem with a judge (who was put in power by the people through the law) issuing a search warrant. If the magistrate is unfairly treating the individual, then no warrant will be issued, as the law does not permit it.

Essentially, the U.S. Constitution protects your person (you), your houses (land property, place of business), your papers (identification, information, bank account data, etc.), and effects (the items you own) against unreasonable (decided by an elected or appointed judge) searches and seizures. They must have "probable cause" (the definition of which is decided by laws), and they must say what will be searched, who, and what will be taken by the government. As you can see, it is extremely difficult for one person or group of conspirers to penetrate multiple levels of authority to unlawfully persecute a people, group, or individual because the Fourth Amendment will stop them in their tracks 99 percent of the time.

In addition, any information that was extracted unlawfully to build a case against you cannot be used in court. Thus, if you were accused of a crime and an officer had not obtained a warrant to acquire the evidence that was used against you, then that evidence would be *null and void*.

Indeed, some could advocate that if you aren't doing anything wrong, then you should have nothing to hide. The government could catch many evil criminals if there were no Fourth Amendment, correct?

Our first president, George Washington, comes to mind, when he said,

> *"Government is not reason; it is not eloquent; it is force. Like fire, it is a dangerous servant and a fearful master."*

If you strip the laws away from the average citizen, you should expect criminal and heinous acts by the government. If you strip the laws away from the government, then you would expect mass persecutions, genocide, and anarchy. History has proven this unfortunate fact time and time again. Unchecked governments butchered over 260 million innocent lives in the last century alone.

Allowing the government to sneak and peer into the lives of its citizens without the requirement to follow due process of law is like letting a mad dog off his leash. There will be no limit to who can be targeted and for what reason. Soviet Russia was perhaps the most highly monitored population, as their secret police could take a listen to any conversation, read any correspondence, and judge guilt arbitrarily. Did this help against crime? In fact, it increased the government's capacity for crime, as over 20 million of its citizens were led to the slaughter for their "guilt."

Another basic reason why the Fourth Amendment is so important in the life of a free U.S. citizen is the fact that it walks in step with basic property rights.

James Madison once wrote:

> *In the former sense, a man's land, or merchandize, or money is called his property.*
>
> *In the latter sense, a man has a property in his opinions and the free communication of them.*
>
> *He has a property of peculiar value in his religious opinions, and in the profession and practice dictated by them.*
>
> *He has a property very dear to him in the safety and liberty of his person.*
>
> *He has an equal property in the free use of his faculties and free choice of the objects on which to employ them.*
>
> *In a word, as a man is said to have a right to his property, he may be equally said to have a property in his rights.*

A person's property not only refers to what he or she owns, but who he or she is. Your own conscience, choices, speech, opinions, and beliefs are your personal property. The Magna Carta protected the physical form of personal property, but the Fourth Amendment of the Constitution protects that of the intangible kind.

The U.S. government must move through the proper channels of authority, utilizing due process of law, in order to prosecute a U.S. citizen. Not only does this apply to your house, your car, your coffee maker, and your golf clubs, but it also applies to you as a person.

The Constitution is clear that the government must honor a person's privacy. However, how far from the law have we wandered in this new era?

HOW FAR WE'VE COME

Politicians seem to have fallen in love with the idea of the U.S. being a democracy. Sadly, this nation does indeed resemble more of a democracy than a constitutional republic, especially considering how many of its own laws it continues to violate.

It is becoming apparent that much of the U.S. government is becoming hostile to the privacy of the American people. For example, in 2013, the IRS made headlines for their focused harassment of ideologically conservative political groups, even inquiring of a pro-life organization about the "content of their prayers." In a country where all views should be protected under the First Amendment, this was an unprecedented outrage. Around the same time, the Justice Department came under fire for their wiretapping of several members of the Associated Press. That incident came under congressional investigation.

There certainly is a catastrophic disconnect between what the Constitution allows and what the government is actually doing in this new era of American history. As we continue in following chapters, I will explore just how our information is simply being sold to the highest bidder. The biggest buyer of our personal information has been the U.S. government (to the detriment of our personal liberty, our property, and our privacy).

Also, those folks in the government who illegally seek the private information of law-abiding citizens are not the only criminals involved in this act. Even petty identity thieves have become quite proficient in collecting the good names and information of unwitting victims. These days, personal information is like gold; it is incumbent upon responsible folks to protect that data. Your good name is under attack by criminals of all shapes and sizes. It's time to protect our persons, houses, papers, and effects against those enemies of law and liberty.

Chapter 2

IDENTITY THEFT: THE GRAND SCHEME

Before the information age, it was very difficult to hijack someone else's good name. Folks carried around cash and coin, and most assets were tangible. Communities were smaller and face-to-face business dealings were far more common, thus confidence men (con men) weren't nearly as effective as they are today.

In the last two decades, the Internet has truly changed the world. Now, information can stream to our computer screens with a literal touch of a button. While this convenience has brought about immeasurable progress, it has also opened the Pandora's Box of identity theft.

Through our society's technological advances in business, finance, and information, identity thieves are more enabled than they've ever been. The

simple acquisition of small bits of information can become a gold mine for folks who want to destroy lives to make a buck. There are several methods by which this happens, but for this chapter, we will explore just how extensive the problem has become in the grand scheme. Our goal is to help you understand the severity of the issue and just how real identity theft can become in your life.

IDENTITY THEFT ON A NATIONAL LEVEL

According to the Bureau of Justice's 2008 statistics, it seems that identity theft isn't going away any time soon:

- An estimated 11.7 million persons, representing 5 percent of all persons age 16 or older in the United States, experienced at least one type of identity theft in a two-year period.

- Although the total financial cost of identity theft was nearly $17.3 billion over a two-year period, less than a quarter (23 percent) of identity theft victims suffered an out-of-pocket financial loss from the victimization.

- About 42 percent of victims spent one day or less working to resolve the financial and credit problems associated with the identity theft; however, 3 percent continued to experience problems related to the theft more than six months after discovering it."

With a population of roughly 310 million in the U.S., these statistics say that identity theft victimized about 4 percent of Americans in a two-year period… and this was back in 2008.

According to the Javelin Strategy and Research Report, based on statistics that were published in 2013, the years since 2008 have seen steady and large increases in identity theft.

The numbers are now roughly 12.6 million new cases of identity theft *per year* that are taking place, which means that one identity theft happens every three seconds.

Also, the report emphasizes that identity thieves are getting smarter about their crimes. They have seen a drop in the average length of time that a particular identity is being used, meaning that notifications to the victim are less likely, and the criminal is long gone before the victim knows that the theft had occurred. Essentially, in 2010, the thief would use a victim's identity for ninety-five days. In 2012, that number was down by half to forty-eight days.

Identity thieves have also learned that they are less likely to get burned by avoiding stores with lots of infrastructure in place to catch them. To that end, they've been flocking to smaller mom-and-pop retail businesses. It's becoming clear that this problem is not only here to stay, but also it is on the rise in a big way.

YOUR RISK

According to CreditReport.org, your odds of becoming an identity theft victim are extremely high:

> *The United States Department of Justice states that in 2010, 7 percent of all United States households had at least one member of the family at or over the age of 12 who has been a victim of some sort of identity theft. That means the odds are greatly against you. Identity theft sets the government, American citizens, and businesses back by billions of dollars each year. From 2005 to 2010, 64.1 percent of these instances involved credit card fraud, the fastest growing type of identity theft. Over the range of this time period, credit card misuse was doubled as the determining factor in identity theft.*

Back around the turn of the century, you would hear about identity theft on the news. Around 2008, you would hear about a neighbor dealing with identity theft. Now there's a good chance that someone in your family has had to deal with identity theft. In the near future, you might be next. Here are a few examples of the kinds of identity theft that may take place in your life.

COMMON TYPES OF IDENTITY THEFT

Identity theft can come in many forms, but basically it has to do with the extraction of information that is used in order to steal from the credit or bank accounts of victims. The main reason why identity theft has become one of the most common crimes in the U.S. is because of an identity thief's capacity to take everything from a victim without seeing his or her face, much less holding a gun. This means that the risk vs. profitability ratio has swayed far into the criminal's favor. Stealing from someone without having to look him or her in the eye, with little chance of getting caught by authorities, is always a prime scenario to a thief.

One of the most common types of identity theft happens when a criminal steals *credit card information*. He then uses this credit card information to purchase items, running up the tab on the victim's credit limit.

Also, identity thieves can steal other personal information (such as social security information, dates of birth, addresses, etc.), and then use this information to open up *lines of credit, mortgages, and other types of loans.* Oftentimes, the only way victims find out about the problem is when they try to get a loan and find out that they've been denied due to a tanked credit score.

Other types of identity theft include *grave robbing,* whereby the thief assumes the identity of someone who has been deceased. Not only is this incredibly difficult to detect (since the primary victim is no longer living), but it is often the most profitable for the criminal. The folks that are most affected by this type of identity theft are the ones left managing the estate of the deceased.

Child identity theft has also been on the rise in recent years. This is perhaps the most savage kind of identity theft, since it has the capacity to destroy a person's life while he or she is still in childhood. This type of identity theft is nearly impossible to detect, especially since checking the credit score of children is obviously not a common practice. The only chance the parents can find out that this type of identity theft is taking place against the child is when bank notices arrive in the mail. This, of course, only happens in the event that the child's address, and not a different address, is used.

These are just a few common forms of identity theft that you may want to watch out for. However, be aware that there are far more elaborate schemes that are being used by identity thieves. These schemes can become extremely sophisticated in increasing the thief's ability to extract information, use it, and cover their tracks on the way out, laughing all the way to the bank.

DAMAGES

The damage that can be inflicted by identity theft is sometimes extensive, and often, victims never get their good name back to the way things were before the crime was perpetrated.

This is because the average citizen is inseparably dependent upon his or her identity. We use social security numbers for everything from acquiring a driver's license to applying for a job to taking out a mortgage. In addition, the information age has brought us the cashless society, meaning that access directly into a bank account is easy and happens on a very regular basis. If a debit or credit card has been compromised, then the entire account to which it is connected is compromised as well.

Where once highwaymen could only steal what the victim possessed on his or her person, now identity thieves can make off with entire savings accounts within minutes under cover of Internet cafe IP addresses.

Of course, the larger the amount stolen, the more attention it attracts. Thus, identity thieves prefer to steal small amounts at a time from a large number of victims. This is one reason why most victims never realize that identity theft is occurring in their life. In addition, with the protections many banking and financial institutions put in place, victims don't always suffer immediate out-of-pocket expenses. CreditReport.org states:

> *According to the Federal Trade Commission's 2006 report, while 50 percent of all identity fraud victims accrue little to no out-of-pocket charges for the legal fees, lost wages, and false payments brought upon them during the fraud, a small bracket of 10 percent of all identity theft victims incur considerable out-of-pocket expenses. This can be upwards of $1,200. This is most commonly the case when fraudsters use a false identity to open new accounts. The top percentile of these victims lost as [much] as $3,000, an unsettling amount to personally lose as a result of identity theft. Few things leave a person feeling more vulnerable and taken advantage of. Likewise, resolving identity theft crime isn't easy. Ten percent of all victims spend 55 or more hours sorting out their problems, while the top 5 percent spend at least 130 hours.*

While most folks don't experience any out-of-pocket expenses, the most aggravating expenditure is time and effort to repair and renew broken credit and accounts.

In addition, the general public ends up paying the price. Not only must retail, banking, and financial institutions recuperate their monies by raising rates, but also much of this cost comes out of public treasuries. Often times, the government bails out individuals and businesses that have been affected by identity theft (not to mention the cost involved with tracking and catching identity thieves, which must now be covered by the U.S. taxpayer).

Totaling out the yearly cost of identity theft, the Javelin Strategy and Research report states that $21 billion was stolen in 2012, making identity theft one of the most lucrative and damaging crimes in America.

Don't be a victim.

Chapter 3

CORPORATE THEFT BY CONSENT

It's often a sobering realization to find out what people know about you. In the old days, information about your personal dealings would usually stay within your local area and in your circle of friends and family. Sure, everyone in your place of business, church, or school would know that you lost a job, got engaged, or decided to buy a new car, but that's how it's always been. You knew them and they knew you.

But now, imagine finding out about yourself from folks you've never met. Suddenly, you discover that a person that lives 3,000 miles away knows your name, what you drive, where you went to college, what you do for a living, or where you live. Even more unsettling would be to realize that people around the globe can find out your Social Security number, who your spouse is, your preferences in clothing, where you attend church, and even personal information, such as credit card numbers, medical data, and family history. Welcome to the twenty-first century.

If you use the Internet to purchase, research, work, play, and vent about politics, emotions, and beliefs, then there's a very good chance that you have multiple profiles on you that exist in giant computer servers from different data mining corporations from all over the world.

WHAT IS DATA MINING?

Essentially, corporations that extract, record, catalogue, store, and then sell the personal information of private individuals are considered *data mining companies.*

These corporations keep your information on file as inventory. Next, the data mining companies sell your personal information to other companies who want to target you to market their goods. It has long been known that the best kind of marketing is *targeted marketing,* whereby a company can actually seek out folks who fit the most common demographical profile who buys their goods. This means that, if a data mining company has extracted your information, then there is a very good chance that your personal data has been distributed far and wide.

There's actually a very simple way to know if you are being targeted for marketing—hop online and go to websites that run advertisements. Perhaps the most common types of websites that are most known for this type of marketing are social networking utilities, like Facebook or Twitter. Look at the advertisement banners that are placed in different spots around the screen. Notice anything familiar?

Indeed, that plasma-screen TV you bought online last Wednesday is showing up in those advertisements. Better yet, it's from the same company. Coincidence? I think not.

THE CULPRITS

Before mass networks, virtually unlimited supply of data storage space, and the convenience of the Internet, it was rather difficult to have on file such extensive profiles about consumers. Now, entire corporate empires have been built upon the collection of personal data.

Perhaps the most well-known data mining companies in the world come in the form of those familiar web search pages: Google, Bing, Yahoo, etc.

These companies are able to rake in billions of dollars in revenue by recording what people search for on the Internet. How the search engines make money is through a certain kind of target marketing called *search marketing*.

When you, the consumer, type in the words "Nikon riflescope" in the search bar, you will notice that "sponsored ads" appear at the top of the page from companies that sell Nikon riflescopes. These companies paid Google so that they'd pop up in the search page whenever someone searched certain keywords that pertained to the products that company was selling. Search marketing is considered to be an extremely effective marketing practice because the retailer can target their customers with laser precision, while not wasting time on folks who have absolutely no interest. Search engines can charge premium prices for their highly lucrative service, which is how they've become some of the most successful corporations on the globe. They cut out the middleman, as it were, by bringing both the data miner and the marketing firm under the same corporate roof.

From this ability to record searches and IP addresses, they have been able to build vast stores of information. In fact, Google has even been able to predict flu epidemics based on global trends of searches pertaining to flu symptoms. From this capability, they've detected flu outbreaks even faster than the World Health Organization.

Google.org tells us how they can accomplish such a monumental task:

> *Traditional flu surveillance is very important, but most health agencies focus on a single country or region and only update their estimates once per week. Google Flu Trends is currently available for a number of countries around the world and is updated every day, providing a complement to these existing systems.*

Other types of data mining companies can come in the form of social networking utilities like Facebook, MySpace, or Twitter.

If you use any of these utilities, then not only do the data miners know who you are, but now they know *what you are like* as a person. They don't have to sneak about trying to spy out your personal information—they've found that it was simply easier for the consumer to hand it over willingly.

So, anytime you post a photo, update your status, "like" something, share something, and construct a profile, these social networking utilities receive mountains of information that they can collect and analyze.

These networking utilities store and load your personal information into highly complicated algorithms, based on massive amounts of data they collect on you. Then, businesses that buy personal information from companies like Facebook can do more than run ads based on your Internet searches—they can now do so based on your likes, hopes, dreams, beliefs, and interests. This is an unprecedentedly invasive look into personal information for marketing purposes, so how do they get away with it? The simple answer is that we agreed to it. According to Facebook:

While you are allowing us to use the information we receive about you, you always own all of your information. Your trust is important to us, which is why we don't share information we receive about you with others unless we have:

- Received your permission;

- Given you notice, such as by telling you about it in this policy; or

- Removed your name or any other personally identifying information from it.

So, you own your information…unless you "agreed" to let them use it, says Facebook. In their own *Data Use Policy,* they admit that anything you publicly post on Facebook is fair game for them to use anyway they want (but only if you give them your consent). So, when did you actually agree to let them use your info?

When you originally created your Facebook profile, you had to check the box that stated that you agreed with their terms and conditions. Thus, they had your complete "consent" from the very beginning.

The practice of collecting data on billions worldwide has become such a lucrative, yet secretive, business that several members of Congress have taken notice. While many of these companies claim that they've done nothing wrong, they seem to be playing their cards rather closely to the chest. Kevin Collier of DailyDot.com writes:

> *The eight members of Congress on it resoundingly denounced the companies' responses.*
>
> *They're "only a glimpse of the practices of an industry that has operated in the shadows for years," the Caucus said in a statement, noting that "many questions about how these data brokers operate have been left unanswered."*

YOUR LIFE IN THE CLOUD

Anytime you use a membership card to your local grocery store, sign up for a mailing list, use search engines, open an account, or upload a photo on a social networking utility, you are willingly contributing your personal information to these massive data mining efforts. In this era, it is very difficult to live a civilized life without doing so.

It is a revolutionary new phenomenon, whereby the information of everyday folks can be easily accessed from anywhere in the world. This cloud of data spans far and wide over almost every facet of life, and it only appears to be growing. For the time being, the "cloud" has no central brain of sorts, but what information can be collected is expanding at an alarming pace.

In fact, even utility companies are on the verge of creating a "smart grid" that will have the ability to track how often you use your home appliances from the fridge to the thermostat.

Home appliance manufacturers are saturating the market with products that have the capability of connecting your home to this smart grid matrix. With these smart grid-compatible appliances, your refrigerator can now snitch on you to the power company. CBCNews.com reports:

> *This kind of information could help make a home more efficient in terms of energy consumption, but it would also be tempting information for marketers, governments and even thieves. The Future of Privacy report suggests that extensive information could be gleaned from the grid — everything from when you shower or watch TV to which appliances and gadgets you have in your home, and when you use them.*

The ominous implication is that one day, the power company may not approve of your lifestyle, so then it can either charge you a fee or simply shut off your power entirely as a penalty.

Also, major manufacturers of consumer goods are quickly moving to the practice of installing RFID trackers in their products. For instance, Katherine Albrecht, founder and director of CASPIAN (Consumers Against Supermarket Privacy Invasion and Numbering), reports:

> *A $600 million company called Checkpoint has developed prototype labels containing RFID spychips for Abercrombie & Fitch, Calvin Klein, and Champion sportswear. These tags contain tiny computer chips with unique ID numbers that can be read remotely by anyone with the right equipment.*

It doesn't stop with clothing. Many large retail companies are even trying to track groceries and other perishable consumer goods with RFID trackers. NaturalNews.com writes:

> *It will monitor your calorie intake, show from where your food was sourced, and even let you know when the food in your fridge is about to go bad—these are some of the enticing claims made by the developers of a new system that embeds edible radio frequency identification (RFID) chips directly into food. Its creators insist the technology will revolutionize the way humans eat for the better, but critical-thinking onlookers will recognize the ploy as just another way to track and control human behavior.*

The current trend is that major corporations will soon be able to keep tabs on their products even after they've left the store. Unfortunately, this trend towards a total invasion of personal privacy is on an obvious and catastrophic rise. Not only will these companies be able to know the basics, such as names, addresses, and Social Security numbers, but they will even be able to tell if you're an early riser (based on when you take a shower), or if you've got a late night snack addiction (based on the data collected by RFID trackers in your "smart fridge").

A brave new world is on society's near horizons and consumers are purchasing it on credit.

Chapter 4

THE WATCHFUL BIG BROTHER

The George Orwell novel, 1984, exhibited a dystopian world of tyranny through fear. Progressing through the story, it is important to notice one very simple and obvious undertone: surveillance.

The main character, Winston Smith, lived in a time when every single action of the individual was under paralyzing scrutiny. Privacy, an idea of a world long gone, becomes obsolete in a world of "Telescreens," microphones, and spies. Indeed, society had parted ways with its intellect and threat of "war" had kept the population in complete obedience. None of this was possible without government officials maintaining an ability to keep tabs on their serfs. In other words, these criminal leaders kept their subjects in line by gaining power through the monitoring of all aspects of individuals' lives.

When a government establishes tyranny, it moves to a de-facto state of war against its own people, *which is why its police force more closely resembles an occupying military.* In war, it is absolutely critical for militaries to spy on their enemies.

This military principle of extracting intelligence before deploying forces is ancient. In fact, in the military classic from 206 BC, *Sun Tzu: The Art of War,* the author writes:

> *Whether the object be to crush an army, to storm a city, or to assassinate an individual, it is always necessary to begin by finding out the names of the attendants, the aides-de-camp, and door-keepers and sentries of the general in command. Our spies must be commissioned to ascertain these.*

Sending spies before the army has been the *modus operandi* (i.e., mode of operation) of militaries since the inception of governments using force. Whether that government is going to war with another nation or it's going to war with its own, it must collect intelligence against its enemies.

This is why you will never find a tyrannical government that does not place its population under heavy surveillance.

In order to entertain the opposing thought process, we must ask the essential question: why would a government ever need to collect mass amounts of data on its own people? Simply put, if the government is doing its job, then a massive surveillance effort is not necessary, as there should be no threat of insurrection.

With the understanding that some small-scale surveillance is necessary in order to keep crime at bay, we pursue the question of when it becomes inappropriate. These surveillance efforts should be subject to the law of the land, in this case the Fourth Amendment. Due process of law is absolutely critical for ensuring that government is not over-stepping its boundaries within its surveillance operations. In other words, these operations must remain within the confines of crime-fighting efforts.

To recap, a military must send spies to collect intelligence before it sends troops into harm's way. In the same way, a militarized police force in a tyrannical state must employ surveillance in order to collect intelligence on the population. The unsettling similarity between both scenarios is that both need to collect intelligence on their *enemies.*

Indeed, in a police state, the general populace is the *enemy* of the governing power. It is important to keep these things in mind when our existing government claims to engage in mass surveillance of the population *for our own protection.*

This is *not* to say that our current government has fully established a police state, though there are certainly subtle evidences that one is being constructed. The problem is that there may come a day when unabashed tyrants blatantly control the U.S. government. They will already have the necessary surveillance infrastructure in place to effectively spy upon the American people if current trends continue.

And the trends seem to be picking up the pace…

DRONES: SCOURGE OF THE SKIES

UAVs (Unmanned Aerial Vehicles), otherwise known as drones, first appeared overseas for intelligence gathering operations in warzones. It wasn't long before the U.S. military weaponized these devices, equipping them with GPS-

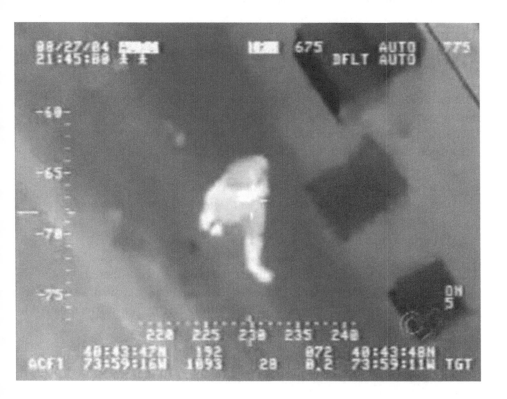

guided missiles. Once the feds began to savor the taste of quick, cheap terrorist assassination capabilities, there was no going back. CNN soon aired pictures of lifeless bodies of terrorists and innocent civilians, as sometimes Predator drones inflict unfortunate collateral damage. The Pentagon had created a monster with a thirst for blood, whether combatant or not.

Shortly thereafter, the scourge of the skies made its way to American airspace. According to Anna Mulrine of *The Christian Science Monitor,* hundreds of drones have already been deployed over the U.S.:

> *Even before that, the number of permits, known as certificates of authorization (COAs), that the FAA issued to organizations to fly UAVs more than doubled from 146 in 2009 to 313 in 2011. As of February 2013 there were 327 active COAs.*
>
> *The bulk of these permits go to the U.S. military for training, and the Pentagon expects their numbers to grow considerably in the years to come. According to a March 2011 Pentagon estimate, the Department of Defense will have 197 drones at 105 U.S. bases by 2015.*

The article also states that the current generation of domestically used drones already has the capability of "see-through" technology, thermal imaging, night vision, and "long-range cameras that can read license plates."

The future of drone usage is still uncertain, but the trend is becoming dark for the personal liberties of U.S. citizens. With the passage of the NDAA [National Defense Authorization Act], the feds can now target American citizens on American soil. Chris Anders of ACLU.org reports:

> *In support of this harmful bill, Sen. Lindsey Graham (R-S.C.) explained that the bill will "basically say in law for the first time that the homeland is part of the battlefield" and people can be imprisoned without charge or trial "American citizen or not."*

The U.S. government has already utilized the power to assassinate U.S. citizens. In 2011, UAV Predator drones executed an air strike against the well-known terrorist Anwar al-Awlaki and killed him. The man just so happened to be an American.

While Anwar al-Awlaki was certainly a dangerous person, the implications of the U.S. government's new power are frightening, and there are now a few essential questions that informed citizens should ask. Where does the trend stop? What is in place to keep the U.S. government from simply labeling American citizens as terrorists, just so they can strip us of our constitutional protections? Since our back yards are considered the new "battlefield," what provisions of law are going to bar the U.S. government from assassinating U.S. citizens on American soil? Lastly, which demographic, ideology, or way of life is next to be assigned the label of "terrorist?"

It is becoming clear that military operators and law enforcement are moving to a remote-controlled battlefield at a breakneck pace, and now, Americans are no longer exempt from being combatants in the warzone. In a world of drones, the Fourth Amendment has been effectively nullified. Sadly, the killing of other human beings has become very convenient, especially when sitting at a desk with a joystick behind a screen.

When your targets can be eliminated with the push of a button, moral obligations are very easily forgotten.

The effects that domestically used UAVs have upon constitutional protections are cancerous; however, these devices are merely tools in the mass grid of technology that is currently being constructed. Orwell's nightmarish vision of *1984* pales in comparison to the surveillance grid that is being erected in the twenty-first century.

ORWELLIAN GRID

Technology is a double-edged sword. Indeed, it can make life more convenient, adding comfort and efficiency to our lives, but it can also be used to spy and track unsuspecting, innocent Americans. Without a certain measure of technology such as cell phones, cars, computers, and credit cards, life in society becomes nearly impossible. Unfortunately, these conveniences are precisely what the government is using to extract surveillance information from the general populace.

Not only do corporations actively peer into the lives of Americans (as we mentioned in chapter 3), but the government has almost attained carte blanche in how deeply it can investigate a person without due process of law. As the government continues to ignore the protections and intent of the U.S. Constitution, spying on individuals is becoming quite easy to do.

Here are just a few ways that the U.S. government is able to track, trace, spy, and surveil:

- If you have a cell phone, the government can pinpoint your location at any time without obtaining a warrant.

- Your cell phone can be used as a listening device, even if it is switched off. This method is called the *roving bug*.

- In many states, citizens must be fingerprinted in order to obtain a driver's license. With this biometric information, the government can track everything a law-abiding citizen touches, connecting a print with a Social Security number.

- Cities and towns across America are installing cameras that can read license plates at intersections.

- Drones are currently being used by law enforcement as surveillance devices.

- The rate of new CCTV camera installations is increasing. Since the Boston bombing of 2013, that pace is rising exponentially.

These are only a few examples of how federal and state governments are able to keep tabs on Americans.

While much of this surveillance will be conducted in the name of fighting crime and terrorists, the most invasive and widespread spying is tax-related. When the IRS investigates individuals, the agency has unprecedented freedom in how deeply it can snoop without having to jump through legal hoops. In addition, some tactics that the IRS has at its disposal resemble the worst kinds of tyranny.

For instance, the IRS is playing Americans against one another through their snitching programs. Consumerist.com reports:

> *If you know someone is cheating on their taxes and your pulse quickens at the thought of the IRS paying **you**, then check out the IRS Whistleblower – Informant Award program. It's a program that rewards you for providing "specific and credible information" that the IRS can use to collect "taxes, penalties, interest, and other amounts" from a cheat.*

Also, the IRS is able to read the personal emails of unsuspecting Americans without the need to obtain a warrant. According to Elizabeth Flock of USNews.com, the IRS sent a memo to special investigation teams. The leaked memo stated: ""non-consensual monitoring of electronic communications... can be used to investigate any federal felony." This memo caught the eye of quite a few lawmakers on Capitol Hill, which caused a full-blown investigation to immerge in 2013.

Also in 2013, the IRS was caught harassing and unfairly investigating ideologically conservative political groups, while giving more liberal groups a pass. In fact, the IRS started asking inappropriately invasive questions concerning the religious beliefs of a certain pro-life group. Charlie Spiering of *The Examiner* writes:

> During a House Ways and Means Committee hearing today, Rep. Aaron Schock, R-Ill., grilled outgoing IRS commissioner Steven Miller about the IRS targeting a pro-life group in Iowa.

> "Their question, specifically asked from the IRS to the Coalition for Life of Iowa: 'Please detail the content of the members of your organization's prayers,'" Schock declared.

Indeed, the IRS thought that the "content of the members of your organization's prayers" were its business.

Also, the IRS is quickly becoming the new lawman in enforcing intrusive government programs. With the passage of the ACA [Affordable Care Act], otherwise known as Obamacare, the IRS received staggering new powers to intrude into the lives of U.S. citizens. Mark Koba of CNBC.com writes:

> "The impact of the IRS on health-care reform is huge," said Paul Hamburger, a partner and employee benefits lawyer at Proskauer.

> "Other agencies like Social Security will be checking for mistakes, but the IRS is the key enforcer," Hamburger said. "It's also going to help manage who might get health care."

With the IRS as the enforcement arm of the ACA, essentially the taxman takes control of your healthcare. Questions begin to arise concerning the

IRS's new role. We already know that the IRS will implement a tax/fee if an American does not purchase healthcare coverage. But, will the IRS ever be able to deny health coverage to compensate for back taxes? They already garnish wages, drain bank accounts, and even go after personal property. What would stop them from penalizing an individual through medical coverage cuts? In the government's perspective, what better way to make sure that tax monies will flow if Americans are worried about the IRS penalizing their health care coverage?

This is precisely why the IRS is becoming the most powerful agency in the lives of U.S. citizens. Not only can the taxman leave you penniless without a home, but now they are involved in your medical care.

Historically, the issue of taxation and money has been the most prevalent cause of revolutions. Thus, it is no accident that perhaps the most hostile and powerful agency in the federal government happens to be the one that collects the taxes. Every American is subject to some kind of taxation, and it is for this reason that the IRS has perhaps the most freedom and power to surveil the public on an individual level.

Some lawmakers are even considering using taxation as a way to place a GPS tracker in your vehicle. This effort will make its debut in the state of California. AOL Autos reports:

> The Metropolitan Transportation Commission of San Francisco is behind the idea and has said that the tax would work by installing GPS units into cars to track the miles that they travel. The vehicle owners would then be charged accordingly, with low-income drivers exempted.

In a police state, the government must control the movements of their subjects. What better way to do so than to make traveling cost prohibitive?

Another possibility is that the state of California would partner with insurance companies that already install GPS devices in cars. One day, your car insurance company could snitch on you to the Internal Revenue Service.

CORPORATE SNITCHES

As we discussed in chapter 3, corporations have the most comprehensive and intrusive information profiles on individuals. The U.S. government is still considerably restricted on how much information it can extract because there remains a small level of protection from the Constitution. In addition, the media diligently jumps on unlawful privacy violations wherever they arise. So, what are the feds to do if they feel so inclined to collect personal data on Americans?

They purchase it.

In the same way that the government would utilize car insurance companies to acquire GPS data to tax individuals by how much they drive, the feds have been partnering with data mining companies and purchasing the personal information of law-abiding citizens. *The Washington Post* reported in 2006:

> *Industry executives, analysts and watchdog groups say the federal government has significantly increased what it spends to buy personal data from the private sector, along with the software to make sense of it, since the Sept. 11, 2001, attacks. They expect the sums to keep rising far into the future.*

Privacy advocates say the practice exposes ordinary people to ever more scrutiny by authorities while skirting legal protections designed to limit the government's collection and use of personal data.

Google admits in their own "Transparency Report" that it has complied with 8438 requests for user information between December 2011 and July of 2012. Despite public outcry, the trend of requests only appears to be on the rise.

With the Constitution out of the way and a nearly unlimited supply of personal information that can be acquired from data mining companies, the government can simply throw the Fourth Amendment to the wind. If the surveillance target ever uses a computer, logs on to Facebook, has an email account, etc., then all constitutional protections are dissolved. The government can find out basic data, as well as very intimate, private data on individuals. Again, the implications of these powers are frightening.

SURVEILLANCE ATTACK

Imagine a day when the government has fully implemented their surveillance capabilities in your life. Let's say that you are the target because of your involvement in a pro-life movement.

On your way to work in the morning, your license plate was tracked every time you went through an intersection. Because of a data request, they were also able to locate your cell phone as well. Once you arrived at work, you logged on to Facebook before the official workday began. You update your status and confirm that you will be attending a pro-life march this evening after work. The government receives that information from Facebook through another data request. They also take note that you Googled the search term, "Ruger SR9 pistol."

Once the workday has ended, you drive directly to the march. At the event you notice small remote-controlled helicopters circling overhead. They take your photo while you are at the pro-life rally. They also take photos of the folks with whom you are associated, your husband, and your daughter. Of course, they already know your friends and family through Facebook, but they are simply confirming that you had actually attended the event.

They accomplished all of this without obtaining a warrant.

Now, let's explore the worst case scenario:

> *During the night, the president signs an executive order stating that pro-life groups are considered terrorist organizations. The provision also gives the Department of Homeland Security unlimited ability to collaborate with the IRS.*
>
> *Your bank accounts are frozen and audited. The fact that you searched for a handgun on the Internet places you in the category of being an enemy combatant. Your medical coverage is cut. Because they have photo evidence of your attendance at the pro-life rally the day before, a UAV is deployed to your location by tracking your cell phone. The UAV follows your movements all the way to work the next morning and you are detained on site. No Miranda rights are read because you are a terrorist.*

Please remember, this is all "for your protection."

In the next section, we will discuss the modus operandi of how your information can be extracted by government, corporations, and criminals. The more you know how they can collect your data and what they plan to do with it, the better you can protect yourself.

SECTION TWO

The Predator's Methods

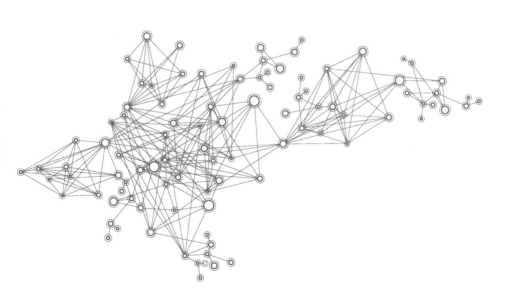

Chapter 5

IDENTITY THEFT TACTICS

As we discussed in chapter 2, identity theft is quickly becoming the favored method among tech-savvy criminals. Perhaps the biggest reason for this is because identity theft can be committed without ever having to look the victim in the eye or setting foot in the victim's home. When a predator can simply extract small fortunes from his or her prey with the touch of a button or the swipe of a card, it spells impending disaster for the rest of us. Identity theft can permanently destroy lives and peace of mind, and with more and more cases of this crime on the rise, it is incumbent upon responsible citizens to prepare and refuse to be victims.

For this reason, we must know what identity thieves are going to do before they carry it out. Learning the predator's methods is the first step in never becoming prey.

METHODS OF STEALTH

Almost all cases of identity theft share a common thread: stealth. It is actually quite easy to prevent identity theft from happening if the victim sees it coming. With a few simple phone calls, the criminal will be stopped in his or her tracks and perhaps prosecuted.

The key for identity thieves to successfully perpetrate these crimes is to make sure that they are not seen approaching and carrying out their methods. If they can steal and use your identity without you ever knowing it, then they've successfully achieved their goals.

Below are several methods that you should know so that you can prevent identity theft from happening in your life.

THE SMALL GAME

A very common practice among identity criminals is to steal small amounts at a time, as it is very easy to detect a large, fraudulent transaction. In fact, most banks will alert you in the event that suspicious transactions are taking place. The problem is that in many cases, no alert will be triggered if the transaction is too small. If the identity thief is crafty, he or she will be able to get away with the scam without the bank or the account holder ever knowing it occurred.

However, the first step in making small, fraudulent transactions is acquiring credit card or bank account information. Unfortunately, it isn't always difficult for a fraudster to skim this information from unwitting victims, especially if he or she works in an industry that takes in this data on a regular basis.

For instance, the food service industry is ripe for such problems, as credit cards are regularly changing hands from patrons to the staff. If the restaurant is not actively monitoring for these problems, a fraudster can copy your credit card information within seconds.

In addition, we are often put in a position where it is necessary to give credit card or bank account information over the phone. It is best if you can avoid such a situation, but if not, it is then important that you take steps to protect yourself.

Keep an eye on your credit score and bank statements. You are always the last line of defense against your accounts and good name from being hijacked.

HIGH TECH METHODS

It's not always necessary for an identity thief to handle your credit card in order to extract your valuable information. In fact, all they really need to do is walk near you.

Using equipment that can be bought online rather cheaply, a thief can steal your credit card info remotely. According to Andy Greenberg of *Forbes,* this method can be extremely effective:

> *At the Shmoocon hacker conference, Paget aimed to indisputably prove what hackers have long known and the payment card industry has repeatedly downplayed and denied: That RFID-enabled credit card data can be easily, cheaply, and undetectably stolen and used for fraudulent transactions. With a Vivotech RFID credit card reader she bought on eBay for $50, Paget wirelessly read a volunteer's credit card onstage and obtained the card's number and expiration date, along with the one-time CVV number used by contactless cards to authenticate payments.*

If you have a credit card that can be read from the embedded RFID, then you are already placing yourself at incredible risk.

Another invasive method used by identity thieves is called *skimming*. Essentially, the thief will install a device on ATM machines that will collect debit card information. Then, after a long day of skimming the valuable data off the debit cards of unsuspecting ATM users, the thief will return and retrieve the device, along with possibly hundreds of debit card numbers with it.

However, this is considered quite a risky move for fraudsters, as current ATMs tend to be rather hardened against such methods. In addition, this method forces the thief to return to the scene of the crime. This is why there are usually only a handful of reports per year involving the skimming method.

Nevertheless, you should be aware of suspicious devices before you use an ATM. While you may not actually be able to detect a foreign device, go with your gut. If you see something that appears to be amiss with the ATM, then don't use it!

CONVENTIONAL IDENTITY THEFT

Perhaps, the most common types of identity theft are the methods that involve the victims simply handing over their information. In addition, fraudsters will try propositioning large groups of people at one time. The reason for this is that most folks are going to smell the scam, which means that only a small percentage will fall for it. The more people the scammer can approach, the more personal data they can extract.

For example, if the scammer successfully acquires the personal information of one hundred or so victims, then the payout will be quite lucrative. Thus, if that scammer only extracts $5.00 per month per victim, multiplied by 100 victims, then he or she was able to steal a total of $500 per month. This is why identity thieves prefer having many victims, but only stealing small amounts from each. Another added benefit is that most folks won't call the police over a small amount, which means that it dramatically lessens the risk of getting caught for the identity thief.

Phishing is by far the most common method used in order to extract the personal information of unwitting victims. Essentially, the scammer will send emails or trigger pop-ups to large masses of people. Sometimes, their proposition-base will be in the hundreds of thousands, if the scammer is using an autoresponder program.

In a successful attempt, the scammer will con the victim into giving over personal information, such as credit card data, Social Security numbers, etc., by filling out some kind of an online form. The thief will do this by making the victim believe that the scammer is representing a financial institution, insurance firm, or anything that appears to be a real company or organization.

Of course, the scammer then uses that information for nefarious purposes and the victim is none the wiser.

There are also less technological methods that scammers use, such as utilizing change of address forms issued by the U.S. Postal Service. Essentially, the scammer will divert the victim's mail to an address of the scammer's choice. Once the mail starts rolling in, the scammer must act quickly to take advantage of the information he or she acquires, as it will not be long before the victim realizes that something has gone wrong. This method can be incredibly damaging over a short period of time, as the information that can be extracted is highly valuable.

There are also many other scamming methods that move along these same lines, such as special offers from phony companies and employment opportunities that are sent to you via email, pop-up, or conventional mail. While we will discuss methods of protecting yourself in following chapters, we must emphasize that any employer that requires credit card information is no employer at all. Be aware of this method.

One method that is on a drastic rise is when scammers utilize social networking utilities to extract information. Utilities such as Facebook offer scammers two types of information that they can acquire. First, it offers the ability for the identity thief to utilize phishing-style scams by posing as businesses or organizations, so that the victim hands over personal data. Second, it allows the scammer to know *exactly* whom they are dealing with, based on the extensive personal information that is often shared on Facebook profiles. This provides the scammer with a very well-rounded idea about exactly how best to approach the victim and then heist their identity effectively.

THE SMASH AND GRAB

Obviously, an identity thief can acquire your personal information through simply breaking in to your home or snatching a purse. This is perhaps a method used by the less sophisticated among identity thieves for the simple fact that it carries the highest risk versus the lowest rewards. Then again, it is a method that doesn't require a great deal of planning to accomplish.

Another more simpler, primitive method that scammers use is *dumpster diving*. While most dumpster divers are looking for an old book shelf that was thrown away last weekend, identity thief dumpster divers are searching for old documents, correspondence, and anything else they might be able to use in order to hijack a victim's identity. This method carries perhaps the highest measure of stealth, but the lowest probability of finding anything useful. Especially with folks adopting the practice of shredding documents and credit cards, it is slowly becoming obsolete.

Perhaps the simplest method of extracting personal information is called *shoulder surfing*. Basically, the scammer simply peers over the shoulders of folks who are looking at their personal information in public. While this method of acquiring personal data is very simple, it requires a very high amount of skill in order to execute. Not only does the identity thief need to be able to read and remember numbers quickly, but also read people with accuracy. Simply, if you are in public, be aware of your surroundings if you expose documents and cards that contain your valuable personal data.

DAMAGE INFLICTED

As we mentioned in chapter 2, identity theft can cause massive amounts of damage to the credit and good names of its victims. While the monetary measure of damage can vary from case to case, perhaps the most common aggravation comes in the form of the time it takes in stopping the theft from occurring and moving everything back to normal.

Essentially, once you've identified that you are, in fact, a victim of identity theft, your entire life is put on hold. You must realize that nothing is safe, because you don't know exactly to what extent your information has been compromised.

Here are several actions that you will have to take in order to ensure that the identity theft is stopped in its tracks:

- Cancel all of your credit cards
- Call credit-reporting agencies and file a report. (Equifax, Experian, and TransUnion)
- Close your bank accounts
- Contact your local police and file a report.
- Cancel your online accounts and set up new ones with different passwords and usernames.
- Shred documentation from old accounts.
- Contact companies that may have been part of fraudulent transactions.
- Attempt to identify the leak in your personal information.
- Depending on the financial damage, attempt to recoup the monies that were lost.

In the event that you lost a substantial sum of money, there may be a chance that you might not be compensated.

Perhaps one of the most damaging aspects of identity theft is that of the psychological kind. According to MedicalXpress.com the effects can last long past the identity theft event:

> *"It was very clear that most participants in the study no longer felt safe conducting everyday financial transactions that most of us take for granted," says Van Vliet. Most of the identity theft victims felt they were taking appropriate precautions to safeguard their personal information and had no idea of how that data fell into the wrong hands. The lack of specifics makes it difficult for identity theft victims to attain any closure and move forward. "No matter how well they monitor their financial records for the rest of their lives, they may still feel vulnerable," Van Vliet says.*

Identity theft victims often feel violated and incredibly vulnerable for a very long time afterwards. Some never get over being a victim for the rest of their lives, depending on how personal and extensive the damage was.

Being a victim of identity theft will cost more than just money; it will cost you peace of mind.

In following chapters we will be discussing more specifically what identity thieves are looking for, and later, how to protect that information from falling into the wrong hands.

Chapter 6

THE CORPORATE DATA FARM: HOW THEY HARVEST

In chapter 3, we discussed how data mining corporations have begun the massive undertaking of building extensive profiles on Americans for marketing and other purposes. In addition, we also explored how even utility companies are peeking invasively into homes to which they provide power. We also discussed how RFID tracking devices are being installed in products from perishable groceries to clothing. The effort to peer into the most intimate details of our lives has long been underway and increasing in pace.

We are now going to discuss the methods that corporations use to track consumers. Whether you are working for a company or you are simply buying from them, they want to know your most intimate life details. Also, we are going talk about when private information gets extracted, where it goes, and then who eventually buys it. At the end of the day, it's all about dollars and often, the government is the highest bidder.

THE SNOOPERS AT WORK

Ultimately, the end goal in any corporate effort to extract and analyze consumer information is motivated by the profit. First, companies use consumer data in order to employ *targeted marketing,* as discussed in chapter 3. Second, companies use data mining and reporting bureaus in order to *manage risk.*

Your credit score is much like your life's report card to many institutions. In this era, if your credit score has been suffering due to the recent difficult economic times, it may take a major toll on your overall quality of life in ways you may not have expected. For instance, employers can even look into your credit history in order to determine whether or not they wish to hire you. In order to accomplish this, employers and other organizations are able to check with three major credit reporting bureaus: Equifax, Experian, and TransUnion.

There are many other companies that operate similarly to these bureaus. Not only is your credit score exposed for the world to see, but also your background, insurance claims, health history, prescription history, rental history, and even product returns are easily accessed by folks who want to do this research on your life. If you are working with a company that reports to any of these bureaus, your information will go on the grid and could remain there for years.

THE "ME" EFFECT

Facebook has been notorious for its utility as a snooping device for employers. In fact, some employers are even requiring the passwords and usernames to employee Facebook accounts. This outrage has cause lawmakers to craft the Password Protection Act of 2012. Dara Kerr of CNet.com reports:

> *Six states have officially made it illegal for employers to ask their workers for passwords to their social media accounts. As of 2013, California and Illinois have joined the ranks of Michigan, New Jersey, Maryland, and Delaware in passing state laws against the practice...*

For some reason, federal lawmakers have dragged their feet on the Password Protection Act, which forced these six states to act. It is uncertain why the act never hit the ground running in Washington, especially since voters would see that as a step in the right direction to protect privacy from unreasonable employer requests.

Indeed, there does need to be some level of trust between individuals and corporations; however, the line that divides common-sense practices and the absurd continues to blur and move in the wrong direction.

At the same time, individual consumers are not making it easier on themselves to remain unaffected by this unrelenting snooping effort. With the rise of social networking utilities, individuals are simply posting their personal information online for the world to see. Millennials, otherwise known as the "Me Generation," are willing to publish intimate life details, whereas previous generations would never have dreamed of doing so.

Whether social networking utilities are a natural byproduct of a highly narcissistic generation or companies like Facebook have simply changed the way we look at privacy, we are faced with an unfortunate truth: our privacy will be invaded, because we allowed it to happen…

…one status update at a time.

INFORMATION EXTRACTED BY STEALTH (SORT OF)

When browsing online, your web history can divulge mountains of information about you. Companies can employ various snooping tactics that can be used to track individual users even down to their home address. At this time, most companies are only using this information to gather generalized statistics that help their marketing efforts. Nevertheless, the capability to target individual consumers is already in place.

Most of the time, companies track web browsers by storing *cookies* on those browsers. Essentially, cookies are markers that websites can attach to your browser that allow the website to know it is you when you return. From cookies, companies can determine who you are (especially if you've set up an account with them), how long you stayed, and where you went. In addition, companies can also determine your geographical location through your IP address, which can also be used as a second confirmation of your Internet cookies.

These tracking devices are basically used as a "bug" on your computer. The point is that they want the ability to gain overall statistical information on their web traffic, and they also want the ability to employ targeted marketing on individual users, as discussed in Chapter 3.

Perhaps the most unsettling capability that some of the more advanced websites (Facebook, Google, Bing, etc.) possess is the fact that they can scour your web history. Through Java Script and Cascading Style Sheets (CSS), they can determine where you've been, especially if you aren't someone who erases your browser history on a regular basis. Companies that utilize these types of tactics have the capability of displaying precision-crafted advertisements based on where you've already been.

Metaphorically, it is like being followed by a spy while you are shopping all day. Then, when you get to the store that the spy works for, they give you little flyers pertaining to the stores you have visited during your shopping spree. It is a tactic that is invasive, yet highly effective.

Of course, not all of us do our shopping in cyberspace. Consumers obviously do far more shopping in the real world, but corporations still want to be able to track each customer by what he or she buys. This is the most prevalent motive behind the development of rewards programs and shopper's club cards. Consumers see it as a way to save on deals and discounts associated with using this membership program, but through this, companies are able to do far more than just attract a few more sales.

With every card or membership issued, there is also an assigned customer tracking number. When you present this card every time you check out, that store knows exactly what you buy and how often. For many companies that have invested big bucks into analyzing the data gained from these programs, they can tell what kind of a person you are, whether you like it or not. Target is one such company.

Charles Duhigg of the *New York Times* writes, concerning Target's ability to track individual customers' buying habits:

> The desire to collect information on customers is not new for Target or any other large retailer, of course. For decades, Target has collected vast amounts of data on every person who regularly walks into one of its stores. Whenever possible, Target assigns each shopper a unique code—known internally as the Guest ID number—that keeps tabs on everything they buy. "If you use a credit card or a coupon, or fill out a survey, or mail in a refund, or call the customer help line, or open an e-mail we've sent you or visit our Web site, we'll record it and link it to your Guest ID," Pole said. "We want to know everything we can."

In fact, Target even has the capability of telling which one of their customers is pregnant. Duhigg writes:

> *"We knew that if we could identify them in their second trimester, there's a good chance we could capture them for years," Pole told me."*

It wasn't long before Target ordered their marketing professionals to stop talking to *The New York Times* for obvious reasons.

At the end of the day, we've still allowed such companies to learn the details of our personal lives. They do not force consumers to give up this information unwillingly; instead, they simply coax us into handing it over through clever tactics and secrets of the trade.

THE LIFE OF INFORMATION

It is said that personal information that is recorded and stored by companies is like plutonium: it never goes away, and it can be dangerous for a very long time. However, it has a starting point, and it almost always ends up somewhere. For instance, let's say that you've Google' the search term "church groups."

If you are currently logged into your Gmail account, then Google has not only recorded that search term into your profile, but they also know exactly in what geographical location the search term originated from through your IP address. Before you know it, you begin to find advertisements and videos pertaining to churches in anything that carries a Google account, as Google has stored HTTP cookies in your browser program.

Your long rap sheet of Google searches will reflect in your web searches, YouTube videos, Google Maps, etc. Combining your other search terms that included "hunting rifle" and "coffee shop near Boston," they can conclude that you are a churchgoer who is pro-Second Amendment who also enjoys coffee drinks. With enough of these search terms, Google is able to know what you are going to think before you even think it.

This information gets stored into your profile, which is usually created through something like a Gmail account. Through this account, Google already knows your date of birth and your sex. In addition, Google can record your web history, so they know you use Facebook, Twitter, and they already know about your online shopping habits.

With all this information, gathered by only a single company, they've been able to extract mountains of data that will be put through algorithms to find out exactly who you are.

Actively, Google uses your term "church groups" in order to send you advertisements pertaining to these keywords. Passively, Google keeps this information on file, as it is incredibly valuable for resale and also to comply with government requests.

Let us suppose that the U.S. government has decided to make another extremely large buy-up of Google user information. Let us consider what Uncle Sam now has:

- They have your location, which they can track to a specific address
- Your name
- Your date of birth
- Your gender
- The content of your emails
- The content of your searches
- Your Google mapping habits
- Your web history
- They know about your online shopping habits
- If you have an iPhone, they can even tell your real-time location, even when you are not at home,
- They know your general belief system, hopes, dreams, and even vices
- Through highly sophisticated analytics, they can even know your personality

The U.S. government was able to do all this without even obtaining a search warrant. The scary part is the fact that various departments of the U.S. government make these information requests on a very regular basis, and there is no provision on law to stop them.

THE ESCALATION INTO SURVEILLANCE ANARCHY

As we mentioned in previous chapters, the American people have recently discovered that the government has not only been publically "requesting" your information from data mining companies, but they have direct access to service providers in the U.S., which is a blatant violation of the Fourth Amendment. In the next chapter, we will discuss what agencies like the NSA have been doing and the implications of these scandalous programs. Essentially, it appears as if the government requests information, which should have little public backlash. However, it simply accesses information that could be viewed as a detestable invasion of privacy.

Through this, we know that if the government ever discarded the Constitution and wanted to persecute churchgoers, it would be incredibly easy to locate them…

…because Google was diligent in storing your personal information that the NSA then extracted directly from their servers.

Chapter 7

NSA: WHERE
BIG BROTHER LIVES

Since the beginning of the Obama administration, major public scrutiny into various NSA surveillance programs had somewhat come to a halt. The new president had made eloquent and disarming promises in terms of the way he viewed government invasion of privacy. During the Bush era, the NSA couldn't seem to get away from the public eye, but of course, George W. Bush was a "war-mongering Republican." When "progressive" Obama took office, it was widely viewed that he would bring an end to these Fourth Amendment mutilating programs. American's fears were disarmed and quieted in 2007 when Barack Obama would say things like:

> This Administration also puts forward a false choice between the liberties we cherish and the security we demand…That means no more illegal wire-tapping of American citizens. No more national security letters to spy on citizens who are not suspected of a crime. No more tracking citizens who do nothing more than protest a misguided war. No more ignoring the law when it is inconvenient. That is not who we are. And it is not what is necessary to defeat the terrorists…We will again set an example for the world that the law is not subject to the whims of stubborn rulers, and that justice is not arbitrary.

However, when pressed into a difficult corner, Barack Obama finally came out and said exactly what he thought. Apparently, Bush and Obama have a lot more in common than what we had originally perceived. In response to the Snowden leaks in 2013, Barack Obama said:

> I think it's important to understand that you can't have 100 percent security and then have 100 percent privacy and zero inconvenience. We're going to have to make some choices as a society.

Sadly, this era in American history has shown us that there is a big difference between what a president says and what a president actually *does*.

Since September 11, 2001, the U.S. government has been able to vastly expand its military-industrial and surveillance infrastructure. In the name of fighting terrorism, we found out that the NSA was engaging in warrantless wire-tapping programs under the Bush administration. Many of us thought that these sorts of shenanigans would have been ended when the Obama administration entered the presidency.

We were wrong.

In fact, there was a certain NSA program that continued from the Bush administration all the way into 2011, over two years into the Obama presidency. The project was called STELLAR WIND. Glenn Greenwald and Spencer Ackerman of *The Guardian* reports:

> *The Obama administration for more than two years permitted the National Security Agency to continue collecting vast amounts of records detailing the email and Internet usage of Americans, according to secret documents obtained by the Guardian.*

> *The documents indicate that under the program, launched in 2001, a federal judge sitting on the secret surveillance panel called the FISA court would approve a bulk collection order for Internet metadata "every 90 days." A senior administration official confirmed the program, stating that it ended in 2011.*

Many details of this program are still shrouded in secrecy, entangled in a web of classified documents, red tape, and blacked out segments. Unfortunately, finding any useful information on any of these programs, especially while they are still in operation, is nearly impossible. The American people are left in quite a pickle. The NSA claims that it's not violating the Fourth Amendment, but at the same time, we are barred from seeing *if it actually isn't.* Any time the American people want to have a look into these classified programs to see if we have anything to worry about, the NSA says, "No, that's classified." Then, they reassure us that all is well, and we are simply sent on our way. Should we merely trust them? Would the Founding Fathers have trusted them? I think the answer to that question is rather obvious.

ALONG COMES SNOWDEN

It was early in the summer of 2013 that a former NSA infrastructure analyst opened the floodgates of classified information to the public. Snowden ripped through the U.S. surveillance establishment naming names, stating dates, and disclosing highly classified programs. What were his reasons? Snowden states:

> *I don't want to live in a society that does these sort of things [surveillance on its citizens]...I do not want to live in a world where everything I do and say is recorded.*

This, of course, sounds like a whistle-blower. How does Barack Obama feel about whistle-blowers? Well, according to Change.gov:

> *Often the best source of information about waste, fraud, and abuse in government is an existing government employee committed to public integrity and willing to speak out. Such acts of courage and patriotism, which can sometimes save lives and often save taxpayer dollars, should be encouraged rather than stifled. We need to empower federal employees as watchdogs of wrongdoing and partners in performance.*

But, what does Obama administration *actually* say about Edward Snowden? It turns out Barack Obama considers Snowden as little more than a "29-year-old hacker," while the U.S. government charges him under the Espionage Act. The man who says he loves whistleblowers and watchdogs downplays him, and he is called a traitor by the establishment. Interestingly enough, the

The National Security Agency

most prolific members from both major parties have shown resentment for Snowden. Not just Democrats have made him an enemy for what he did to Obama's approval rating. Republicans like House Speaker John Boehner have outright said that he's a traitor.

Why is this the case? Logically, it seems to be the establishment, the bigwigs from both parties that are coming together to defend these highly intrusive programs. At the same time, Snowden has the majority of his support from independents, moderates, and civil libertarians. This doesn't sound like a Republican vs. Democrat type of fight, but it rather resembles a fight between the establishment and common American folk who do not wish for the government to snoop into their lives. I find it a curious matter that Edward Snowden received so much bad press for his effort to uphold constitutional law (Fourth Amendment) and assault the rising surveillance state, a state which does not subscribe to laws, but rather tends to break them. It is a very Orwellian principle to punish abiders and protectors of the law, while rewarding those who break and assault it. It seems the U.S. government's understanding of its role in American society has been completely turned on its head.

A LEAK BECOMES A TIDAL WAVE

The floodgates burst open, bringing with it a paradigm shift in how patriotic Americans view the national intelligence gathering apparatus. What Snowden revealed was the fact that the U.S. government, particularly the executive branch, had released this peeping Tom agency into the domestic and international neighborhood.

It was perhaps the most massive intelligence leak in modern history, as Snowden named programs, cooperating entities, even calling out questionable spying programs on U.S. allies. In addition, the massive scale of the snooping was far greater than anyone had originally suspected. Once Snowden had released the initial leaks, it became clear that something had gone terribly wrong.

From all that has transpired since the summer of 2013, what do we know now about the intelligence community?

- We now know that the NSA has been actively involved in a full-on cyber war with not-so-friendly countries…and even the friendly ally ones. The NSA has been involved in the unsanctioned monitoring, tampering, and hacking of countries from the UK to China.

o **According to *The Guardian*, the NSA used various tactics against foreign embassies:** "One document lists 38 embassies and missions, describing them as targets. It details an extraordinary range of spying methods used against each target, from bugs implanted in electronic communications gear to taps into cables to the collection of transmissions with specialized antennae."

Edward Snowden

o **The U.S. is heavily spying on the European Union.** Snowden's leaked documents revealed that the U.S. was engaging in Cold War-style snooping. When EU leadership caught wind of these NSA programs, it even began to strain U.S.-EU foreign policy.

o **The NSA has been hacking Chinese servers.** U.S.-Chinese foreign policy has been particularly cold lately, especially concerning the subject of cyber security and bilateral compliance on the issue. However, Snowden unleashed fury upon U.S. foreign relations with China because it was clear that the NSA was hacking Chinese research centers. *South China Morning Post* reports: "The information also showed that the attacks on Tsinghua University were intensive and concerted efforts. In one single day of January, at least 63 computers and servers in Tsinghua University have been hacked by the NSA."

o **The UK's Government Communications Headquarters (GCHQ) was monitoring the members of the G20 to achieve diplomatic advantage. Also, the NSA and GCHQ have been sharing everything...and we mean everything.** Apparently, the UK has had a nasty little habit of spying on their friends, including members of the G20. Of course, to this surveillance-obsessed country, it doesn't seem all that terrible. But, to the rest of the world, this certainly fomented distrust against the country. At the same time, it seems that the cyber relationship between the U.S. and the UK is a blossoming one. With a plethora of fiber optic cables stretching the width of the Atlantic, the info-umbilical cord connects servers from both agencies. The NSA seems to have unfettered access to the GCHQ and vice versa.

- The cat has finally clawed its way out of the bag. The Snowden leaks have displayed to the world that the NSA is spying on American citizens, collecting the data, and storing it in ungodly, massive quantities. In addition, the comprehensive nature of the information is overreaching, and the agency is showing no signs of abating the trend. Also, the NSA seems to have the common misconception that it doesn't have to answer to Congress (or really anyone for that matter.)

  o **According to *The Guardian*, the NSA has been collecting phone record data from major companies such as AT&T, Bellsouth, and Verizon:** "The National Security Agency is currently collecting the telephone records of millions of U.S. customers of Verizon, one of America's largest telecom providers, under a top secret court order issued in April."

  o **One word: PRISM.** It is perhaps the most disturbing revelation on Snowden's leak list, as it details the fact that the NSA has been collecting mountains of data on average-Joe Americans, extracting it directly from those data mining companies we talked about previously. Among the companies you will find YouTube, Skype, Apple, and of course,  Google. The revelation of PRISM made it clear that on the Internet, you are being watched (and remembered).

  o **Two words: Boundless Informant.** The NSA claimed to Congress that it couldn't analyze all the data it extracted through PRISM... but they didn't mention Boundless Informant. The program allows them to analyze what they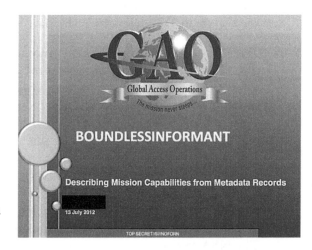

Slide from a presentation

take in from programs like PRISM, which means that they can, in fact, track countless targets. Interestingly enough, from the information derived from Snowden, it appears as if the U.S. is one of the most hotly surveilled countries on their list. According to *The Guardian:* "The National Security Agency has developed a powerful tool for recording and analyzing where its intelligence comes from, raising questions about its repeated assurances to Congress that it cannot keep track of all the surveillance it performs on American communications."

o **We learned that the Obama administration knew about these programs and attempted to mislead the American people.** It appears as if the White House was a bit loose with the truth about these snooping programs. GlobalPost.com reports: "While the documents outline the circumstances the NSA must destroy data collected from U.S. citizens, as well as the rigorous steps analysts are supposed to take to make sure a target is outside the United States, they also reveal several ways the NSA can continue to use data collected on U.S. citizens. The revelations appear to contradict statements by Obama and others that the NSA cannot access data on U.S. citizens without a warrant."

THE AMERICAN ULTIMATUM

Knowing the general content of these leaks, one should ask if Snowden was justified in his actions. The young man did release boatloads of classified information, sending shockwaves through the surveillance community. So, did Snowden do the right thing?

Perhaps a better question is this: who is more dangerous to our life, liberty, and our property? Edward Snowden or the NSA?

These days, it seems quite common for popular support to swing depending on the direction that the mainstream media happens to take the issues. For instance, the overwhelming majority of those in the media are now calling Snowden a traitor. Indeed, support for Snowden has predictably fallen. Even liberal-minded individuals (who would have had a field day if these leaks had taken place under the Bush administration), are largely condemning Snowden's actions. It seems as if public opinion has become like clay in the hands of the establishment, as they are able to guide the American people by the hand, right back into the cage.

Thus, despite the fact that an all-powerful federal surveillance state has grown like a cancer from inside the bureaucratic underbelly of the military-industrial complex, most folks will simply sit back, flip through the channels, and believe that Edward Snowden is a traitor and not a whistleblower…because it's easier. It doesn't matter that an overreaching NSA, *capable* of a mass surveillance program on Americans, is far more dangerous than the man warning us about them. Snowden has fought with words while the U.S. government is now fighting this troublesome whistleblower through the barrel of a gun.

However, debating whether Snowden is guilty or not is still missing the point. The American ultimatum after our most recent discoveries about our government is a simple one. Shall we continue on or shall we return to the way things were?

Because these are the obvious beginnings of a surveillance state, because it is obvious that the U.S. federal government is blatantly ignoring the intent of the Fourth Amendment, because these programs are obviously not in place to stop terrorists, and because it took a "traitor" to reveal the existence of these programs, the answer is in plain sight. There is something terribly wrong happening in the federal government's corridors of power and it must be challenged.

First, there must be a massive effort, spurred along by public outcry, to have these programs stopped until further notice. Second, anyone who lies to Congress on behalf of the intelligence community should be charged with perjury. Third, elected officials should take the reins and investigate these programs in order see the scope of the surveillance, what extent of information is being extracted, and to check for violations of the Fourth Amendment (Hint: saying "that's classified" isn't going to fly). Fourth, all parties involved in illegal activities should be prosecuted. Last, the only way this will ever take place is if the taxpaying voter demands it. Thus, the American people should heap tremendous amounts of pressure upon the White House and both houses of Congress.

At this point, the American people know that the U.S. government is now operating outside the law, gaining tremendous power in the process. There may come a day when the office of the presidency is replaced by a tyrannical faction, and this individual (or group of individuals) will have the ability to monitor every aspect of their citizens' lives. As we discussed earlier, the object of surveillance is to keep watch on *your enemies*. What is in place to stop this from happening? The Constitution. If we ignore the Constitution, then there is nothing standing between the American people and a very difficult road ahead.

If the events of the summer of 2013 do not inspire fundamental and consequential change in public opinion, then America has truly wandered into uncharted territory. If so, let us hope that we may find our way back before we wake up and realize that it is, in fact, too late.

Chapter 8

THE PRESIDENT'S MEN: HOW THE IRS IS CHANGING AMERICA

By definition, the Internal Revenue Service (IRS) should be a mere bureaucracy, possessing no political agenda, only carrying out established policy, and directed by elected officials. While the constitutionality of the IRS as a whole is debatable in a legal sense, the agency should be nothing more than an enforcement arm for the purpose of tax collection, and it should remain completely aloof from political dialogue. Simply put, the IRS has no place in politics, as it should have no opinions of its own. It is a powerful servant, which simply executes policies previously defined by the elected representatives of the people. The IRS should be a tool with no mind of its own.

However, as we mentioned before, the timeless topic of taxation has always been one of the most common issues that start movements and revolutions. Why? It is due to the fact that taxes are what fund governments (thus, a reason why governments need their citizens) and often, taxes are what government uses in order to force its will upon the people (and a result of citizens needing their government).

It is these two principles that have been the cause of tax revolts since as far back as the Egyptians. Even recorded tax wars can be traced back to the Roman Empire and the Jewish zealots of the first century A.D. In fact, the New Testament Christian Bible mentions how adamantly the Jews hated Roman taxation. The popular phrase "So give back to Caesar what is Caesar's, and to God what is God's," comes from the Gospel of Matthew 22:21, as Jesus was commenting on the fact that it is correct for citizens to pay taxes to the government.

Indeed it *is* correct for citizens to pay taxes. Taxes are what fund governments, and strong governments are absolutely necessary to maintain law and order. Without law and order, there can be no economic growth and wealth creation, because there are no laws protecting personal property. Principally, our taxes go to protect our life, liberty, and property. A properly functioning government uses tax monies to safeguard the people who fund it, whilst protecting their prosperity.

This is the reason why the U.S. House of Representatives, the house that is directly and proportionately controlled by the will of the people, possesses the power of the purse. This makes the House arguably the most powerful legislative arm of the U.S. federal government, as they have the ability to control the funding. Without funding, the government cannot operate. With more funding, the government can increase its power and influence. The Constitution places the power of the purse squarely in the hands of the people, which is exactly where it belongs.

This understanding of the awful and useful power of taxation was rather fresh in the minds of the Continental Congress when the U.S. Constitution was being drafted. Indeed, the American War for Independence was largely fought on the basis of unfair taxation and extremely damaging economic policies. In addition, colonial governments that were already in place were being forced to fund an overseas "mother government" that was based in an entirely different hemisphere. The colonial population never stopped funding *their* government.

The War for Independence was not a question of *if* the people should pay taxes, but rather *to whom* the people should pay taxes.

It is easy to understand why governments and their respective populations are constantly on edge in regards to the issue of taxation. Oftentimes, governments are able to set up agencies or middlemen between them and them people. In this era of American history, our tax middleman is an arm of the White House—the IRS.

The IRS we know today was established in 1913 with the ratification of the 16th Amendment, which states that the U.S. government has the ability to tax incomes (interestingly, this was the same year that the Federal Reserve Act was passed, a curious coincidence). As we noted above, the IRS is a middleman, a tool for the feds to collect our tax dollars to pay for the interest on national debt, fund defense spending, fund government programs, etc. Again, the IRS *should* have no agenda. Only elected politicians should have agendas.

Thus, when the IRS was discovered operating on an obvious and active agenda in 2013, it was disturbingly alarming to the average taxpaying citizen. We know that the issue of unfair tax policy is historically the most prevalent cause of revolt, war, and civil unrest. Empires have fallen, regimes have been removed, and blood has run in the streets as a result of grievances on both sides of the issue. From a historical perspective, the gravity of the situation and the results thereof have the potential to alter a nation's course permanently. So, when the taxman chooses a political side, that is when things may become ugly…very ugly indeed.

THE TEA PARTY MOVEMENT

In 2008, the Obama administration assumed control of the executive branch of the U.S. government, backed by ample support from both houses of Congress. Within the first few months, it was rather evident that there would be a difficult conflict between constitutional conservatives and the new administration's far-left-leaning ideologies. In response to the Obama administration's first few actions, the new Tea Party movement began, capturing national attention. The movement seemed to sprout from the grassroots of mainstream America and within a year's time, the effects could be felt in Washington's corridors of power.

The Tea Party movement's primary platform revolved around unfair taxation, as the issue was exacerbated by a deepening recession. The new president insisted upon increasing deficit spending and raising taxes (even while reassuring the U.S. populace that this was not the case). Also, a few establishment Republicans decided to betray conservative ideals by backing the president's measures, and many of them simply decided that it was not politically expedient to come out against them. This led to a feeling of alienation for many constitutional conservatives, naturally uniting many in opposition, and protests began in communities across the entirety of the U.S. under the iconic, yellow Flag of Gadsden (Don't Tread On Me).

The movement took off, aggravating and upsetting the powers-that-be. This new movement had to be demonized, stifled, suffocated, manipulated, and stopped at all costs.

The Tea Party slowly began to lose steam. This was obviously not because the Obama administration relented in its openly socialist policies, and it wasn't even because the Tea Party was losing supporters. For some reason, it seemed that the Tea Party movement wasn't able to become an established force. They were finding it oddly difficult to become political non-profit organizations so that they could raise funding and support for the cause. What was happening? We all found out during the summer of 2013.

THE PRESIDENT'S WAR ON TEA

On May 10, 2013, Lois G. Lerner, a person who oversees the application process for organizations seeking tax-exempt status, officially spilled the beans to the public. *The Washington Post* reported:

> *What we know: In short, the IRS targeted certain conservative groups seeking tax-exempt status for extra scrutiny at beginning in 2010, according to an inspector general's report released last week.*

It became clear that the IRS had, in fact, singled out conservative groups. While these groups were not denied tax-exempt status, they were simply placed on hold. Tax-exempt status allows these groups to acquire funding, giving their supporters a tax break. In addition, it also means that they are exempt from paying taxes, dramatically lowering the cost of operation. In effect, it becomes extremely difficult to run a non-profit organization without this status. So, is it a mere coincidence that tax-exempt status approvals dropped off from 2010 to 2011? *The New York Times* reported:

> *According to the IRS records, 54 organizations were granted 501(c)(4) status since 2010 with "Tea Party," "patriot" or "9/12" in their names. Five of those groups were approved in the first three months of 2010. Approvals then slowed considerably, IRS data shows.*

> *The Indiana Armstrong Patriots was the only Tea Party organization approved during all of 2011, and it was one of just four groups with "Tea Party," "patriot" or "9/12" in their names that were approved from April 2010 through April 2012.*

The IRS even deeply scrutinized and harassed certain religious conservative groups, requiring they answer questions that the IRS had no business asking. One disturbing example regarded a pro-life group. Yahoo News wrote:

> *On June 22, 2009, the Coalition for Life of Iowa received a letter from the IRS office in Cincinnati, Ohio that oversees tax exemptions requesting details about how often members pray and whether their prayers are "considered educational."*

The article continues…

> *"Please explain how all of your activities, including the prayer meetings held outside of Planned Parenthood, are considered educational as defined under 501(c)(3)," reads the letter… "Organizations exempt under 501(c)(3) may present opinions with scientific or medical facts. Please explain in detail the activities at these prayer meetings. Also, please provide the percentage of time your organizations spends on prayer groups as compared with the other activities of the organization."*

The IRS went so far as to ask about the *content of their prayers,* and what percentage of time their organization spent in prayer. No government should ever ask this question to any group or individual, yet the IRS demanded it of a religious group hoping to practice their First Amendment rights. It is a ground-shifting revelation and disturbing at its very core.

Of course, President Barack Obama denied any knowledge of the IRS scandal until the story broke on CNN. However, some Obama administration officials have admitted to knowing that conservative groups were being targeted. In the president's defense, the man may not have known. However, that does not rule out the upper echelons of his administration being aware of the practice.

This does make sense, especially in the world of dirty politics. A politician always wants to avoid the possibility of being forced to lie to the public, as there is always a glaring chance that the lie will come back to them. Thus, it is important for politicians to rely on *plausible deniability,* whilst trusting in their non-elected people to carry out their agendas in the shadows.

In this way, the president may have had a conversation with one of his advisors, saying something along the lines of: I wish you would do something about the tea partiers. At which point, the advisor in some capacity would say: I'll take care of it, Mr. President, while never actually divulging *how* his job would be carried out. Even if the president *could,* he *would not* want to know, which means that he *doesn't have to lie.*

This, of course, is a theory. Nevertheless, my theory is entirely plausible for the simple aspect of the *timing* involved with the IRS scandal. For instance, if one were hoping to start a non-profit organization for the purpose of influencing and campaigning for an upcoming election, then the time to acquire that tax-exempt status would have to be roughly two years before the election takes place. This window is when the majority of funding is raised for campaigning costs.

According to *The New York Times* article, the IRS had generally placed conservative groups on hold from 2010 through 2012. Thus, if upper echelons of the White House directed IRS officials to hold applications and harass these groups during those two years, it is obvious that they were in the active process of influencing the 2012 elections. Thus, it would be no coincidence that in 2013, tax-exempt approvals shot up dramatically for conservative groups, especially since 2012 was the Obama administration's last election.

CONSEQUENCES

At present, we do not (and probably will never) have the entire story in regards to the depth of the IRS scandal. The Obama White House has done a fantastic job at blurring the understanding of who was at fault, who knew about the scandal, and exactly what transpired. Even the IRS has covered its tracks efficiently, burying the dead weight and irrelevant parties before a congressional investigation, while blacking out the rest of the details.

This forces the American people to operate on the improbability of coincidence and the ambiguity of theory.

Understanding this, it seems most probable that the IRS was neck-deep in influencing an American election through the suppression of lawful assembly and free speech under the directive of the Obama White House. If this is actually what transpired, then the U.S. government has truly reached a new low.

This action will set a new precedent in American history, as once apolitical bureaucracies that carried out policies enacted by elected officials are now involved in the unlawful influence of politics through policy. This means that the U.S. government can govern without the consent of the people. Rather, governance will be done through the coercion of the people. It is a revolutionary, tyrannical concept never seen in American history and only seen in despotic regimes throughout world history. In other words, we are becoming Nazi Germany, Communist Russia, and Rome.

The IRS is perhaps the most powerful bureaucracy under the president's control for the simple fact that they are the tax collectors. As we mentioned before, the IRS can influence your health care, your property, your bank account, and they even tax you when you die. Indeed, their power is increasing with every election cycle.

As we continue to connect the dots, the perfect storm for a surveillance state is on approach and increasing speed. We know that the IRS will simply act on presidential orders without any thought to the intent of the Constitution. The NSA and other intelligence collecting entities are actively and closely monitoring the activities of average Americans. Yet the public seems to continue meandering along, docile and unaware at the monumental ramifications of these facts.

In the next chapter, we will paint a picture of these ramifications, pulling together what we now know about the growing surveillance state. At present time, Washington's agencies and services—the arms they use to keep tabs and influence the population—are still broken up. However, when they begin working together closely is when the nightmare will officially begin.

Chapter 9

SURVEILLANCE NIGHTMARE AND THE CONSEQUENCES OF AN UNPROTECTED IDENTITY

In a very real sense, your privacy—your identity—is your life. If your name is compromised, the event can turn your entire world upside down. Your good name is how your fellow man addresses you, and when your identity has fallen into the wrong hands, it can affect relationships, business dealings, and especially your credit.

In addition, your name is your marker, making it easier for you to be tracked, traced, and followed by less-than-benevolent entities. Privacy is about more than just keeping your identity safe and in good standing, as it also concerns keeping it out of sight and anonymous when dealing with corporations and government. Of course, there are certain circumstances that require you to divulge details in your life (taxes, census, citations, state-issued identification, etc.). However, that information is still a far cry from monitoring phone conversations and personal data.

It is important to understand what could be before we attempt to avoid such a disastrous scenario. In this chapter, we will be discussing the ramifications of a stolen identity, and also the difficulties one may face in a surveillance nightmare. These examples imagine the worst-case scenario for both issues.

My aim is that you will understand the importance of protecting and fighting for the anonymity of your identity. This is a glimpse of a world that we foresee in the event the privacy of the individual has been negated and your every detail is exposed for the predators to see. Considering what *could happen* is the first step in stopping the hypothetical worst from occurring.

THE ABSCONDED GOOD NAME

As we previously discussed, wireless, electronic, and digital communications have opened up the individual to a minefield of identity theft possibilities. In addition, identities are highly valuable commodities on the black market. A very common practice among identity thieves is to steal the information of an unsuspecting victim and, rather than using it, the thief will sell it to a buyer (or buyers).

An identity theft often plays out by the victim becoming informed about unauthorized use of their account information after the fact. For instance, you may be simply going about your daily routines when you receive a phone call from your bank. The customer service representative informs you that suspicious activity is taking place on your account, asks you a few questions for verification purposes, and gives you the option of either ignoring the incident (preferably not the option one should take) or the option to freeze the account.

However, not all identity theft takes place in this way. Perhaps the worst-case scenario occurs when a highly proficient identity thief (or someone close to you) is able to acquire your Social Security number and other forms of identification. When this happens, the identity thief can either sell the information, keep it until he or she needs to use it, or begin operating with the information within hours of the information extraction.

If this occurs, it has the potential to be a nightmare. Often times, the individual who has access to your personal information can open lines of credit, mortgages, and even bank accounts. In addition, because the thief is smart enough to know not to use your bank, you will most likely not receive any notification until it is far too late.

Identity thieves will work quickly, as they most often make their play from extraction to aborting the operation within forty-eight hours. This means that if an identity thief opens up a line of credit or a mortgage in your name, then he or she has already absconded with the value from your credit (account withdrawal, purchase of goods, etc.). If you are currently unprotected from such a scenario, then you will most likely not hear about your predicament until you attempt to check your credit score or apply for some kind of loan. Even worse is when you are informed about the problem through collection notices.

Depending on the net worth or credit rating of the victim, the damage could be in the hundreds of thousands of dollars (in a few cases, it could be millions).

Also, it is nearly impossible to determine exactly what information the identity thief possesses.

If you do not know who the thief was or what personal information the thief has taken, then you will have to assume that he or she has everything and no information is safe. The fastest way to stop the leak is to identify the thief. However, this rarely ever happens, as identity thieves have a tendency to cover their tracks quite well (especially if they've dropped the use of the identity within forty-eight hours, indicating their level of skill and experience in the field). In addition, if the identity thief is a family member or friend, then the scenario becomes even more complicated. Making such accusations is never an easy matter.

Also, if the thief was able to find multiple buyers, then there is no telling how many people are operating on your personal information.

In the event that the identity thief cannot be found, you have to assume that all information has been compromised since you may not know what information was extracted. You might be able to change your Social Security number, but if you have not changed your driver's license number, bank account numbers, passwords, and the like, then the thief may still be able to operate on your information.

This is perhaps the trickiest part about being an identity theft victim. While the initial damage may not be extensive, it is the inability to know exactly what information has been compromised so it can be changed to prevent more damage from occurring. Also, the psychological damage can be excruciating, as there are always residual fears that the problem may not have been completely wiped out. Paranoia is a very common emotional issue among identity theft victims, as the loss of peace of mind is almost unavoidable.

In many cases, the total resolution of a single identity theft can take years. The financial and psychological effects can last decades, and overall trust towards family and friends can suffer detrimental effects that may never be reversed. Quality of life may never return to the way it was before the crime, which is why identity theft is known for its total and catastrophic life-altering effects.

For example, if a criminal steals a car, then the victim knows exactly what has been compromised—the car itself and the contents inside at the time of the theft. However, when an identity theft happens, someone steals an entire lifestyle, a lifestyle that was enjoyed by the individual who owned and rightfully possessed it beforehand. Financial credit, accomplishments, wealth, aspirations, possessions, reputations, hopes, dreams, and relationships can all be compromised, and the worst part is the victim may have no clue how, what, when, where, to what extent, or why the identity theft took place.

Of course, this is obviously the worst-case scenario, as most identity theft cases only compromise small parts of the victim's life. Nevertheless, the possibility exists for *everyone* in this era. No demographic is off limits, as victims can range from men to women, the homeless to the extravagantly wealthy, and babies to the elderly and deceased.

However, there are steps one can take in order to prevent these scenarios from ever happening. Your necessary preparations involve both lifestyle changes and investing in certain companies that have the capacity to protect your good name. We will be discussing these steps in the coming sections of this book.

LIFE IN THE BRAVE NEW WORLD

Americans, while we continue to plunge ever towards a surveillance society, are not nearly as surveilled as those in Great Britain. Especially in their densely populated areas, there are multiple cameras on countless street corners. This spectacle would make most American privacy advocates cringe. However, it is a curious thing to watch street interviews of folks in English cities when they are asked about the cameras.

Unbelievably, most remain unaware and immune to the realization that those cameras even exist. To put it plainly, the incremental process for the implementation of a surveillance state is a rather slow but easy one. When it is in place, usual human psyche will do anything to ignore the uncomfortable feeling of being subject to a violating surveillance grid, even to the point of ignoring its existence entirely.

Essentially, this psychological reaction is popularly called the *normalcy bias.* It is a psychological defense that the mind erects to guard the individual's emotional state from obviously disturbing, but necessary realizations. To boil down the normalcy bias metaphorically, it is the act of plunging our heads into the sand away from a frightening but true reality. This defensive reaction *can be* healthy in certain scenarios, allowing folks to carry on with life. However, the normalcy bias was also made famous by being the reaction of many European Jews when Hitler was in power. They told themselves that life would eventually improve, but they were tragically wrong. The sensible reaction would have been to accurately understand and evaluate the situation in order to evacuate Nazi-controlled zones. Millions did not, simply ignoring their better judgment.

In a surveillance nightmare, it is important to understand that no one actually wants to realize that they are being watched on a constant basis. Perhaps the greatest and most useful weapon of the surveillance state is the fear it produces.

No, not *every* individual will remain under constant, penetrating scrutiny, as this would be a logistic impossibility. However, there is always the *possibility* that "they *could be* watching me *now*." Therein lies the fear, the horror, which is the most prolific and saturating quality of an efficiently run surveillance society, enforced by an all-powerful police state, unleashed by politicians crafting tyrannical policies.

However, in the coming American police state, the cameras aren't even scratching the surface to what approaches.

The skies will soon swarm with surveillance drones watching streets, properties, and, with infrared technology, even peering inside buildings. Of course, you won't always be able to look up and spot them, as most will take flight during the night hours. During the day, the authorities will simply trust in the cameras on the streets and their eyes on the ground.

They already own the tech, which allows them to trace your vehicle through intersections, using software that can read license plates. If you were a target, they could easily track your vehicle through your route, patching together the surveilled intersections through which you passed. Drones also have this technology, which means that if you are truly the subject of scrutiny, then simply avoiding watched intersections would be pointless. They already have you, they already know the make and model of your vehicle, and they can even read your registered vehicle identification number through your windshield, using orbiting surveillance satellites.

Even inside your home, we now know that the NSA has been extracting personal data from corporate data mining companies (thank you, Mr. Snowden). As we discussed earlier, these companies have been installing cameras, microphones, and other sensors in home appliances throughout North America, patching them in to the smart-grid. In addition, they also have RFID trackers on consumer goods and waste, which can be read by your smart-appliances.

This is essentially where they would be able to tell if you had something to hide, as they could listen to your kitchen table conversations and even read your facial expressions when you watch your TV and work on your computer. Also, by analyzing your consumption of products and commodities and measuring household waste, they would be able to figure out how many people reside in the home. Thus, the watchers would know if you are hiding someone or are missing someone. An active surveillance grid under a police state would certainly use this technology to catch remaining dissenters within the populace.

Based on the information we heard during the summer of 2013, we know that the U.S. government has the power to listen to your phone calls, read your emails, texts, and even your mail. Also, they can easily track your online surfing habits, not only letting them know facts about your outer self, but also giving them the ability to analyze the most intimate details of your inner self. Through this capacity, a surveillance state would be able to spot a dissenter from a mile off, for the simple fact that their target searched for information or certain products that their analysts have flagged. In addition, they could easily use your profile as leverage, a footing for blackmail, in the event that you tried to upset the established order in some way.

To delve even deeper into the leverage that the surveillance community can gain from these intimate details of the individual, they now have an open view into your medical records. Through the Affordable Care Act, which was passed into law under the Obama White House, the IRS now handles the financial side of the medical industry. Since the president of the United States essentially controls the IRS, the executive branch has effectively taken control over the health and well-being of the American people. There is absolutely nothing stopping the U.S. government from exploiting the medical needs of the citizenry to gain and consolidate power. How?

Since the U.S. government has now set itself up as the financial administrating arm of the medical industry through the IRS, they can restrict and increase insurance coverage wherever it suits them. To loyal subjects, they can increase; to dissenting citizens, they *can* restrict. Since medical care is a necessity, this gives them absolutely tremendous power and influence. Even so, depending on the draconian laws that are in place, they can mandate who is allowed to reproduce or who is allowed to live past a certain age. Their argument for passing these policies will be the endless expenses of medical care, topped off by a utilitarian argument, and sweetened with a dash of "humanitarian" save-the-earth rubbish.

I am well aware that your normalcy bias may kick in after reading the last few paragraphs, but as we discussed in the last chapter, we now know that the IRS works for the president of the United States. They simply follow orders, and whether or not those orders are *constitutional* is a matter that is, simply, irrelevant.

The IRS has always wielded tremendous, and some would argue, unconstitutional power over the American people. They can freeze bank accounts, seize property, garnish wages, and utilize countless other tactics in order to ensure they are paid monies owed. Once constitutional concerns are made null and void, there is nothing from stopping them from doing the same to political, ideological, and religious opponents.

Perhaps the most sobering aspect about this nightmare is the fact that the U.S. government already has the technology and manpower in place to do all these things.

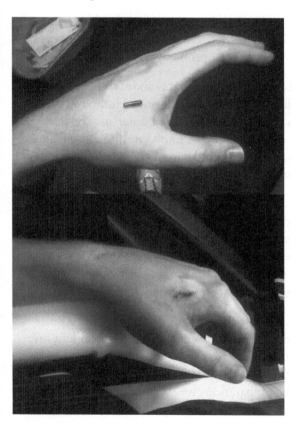

RFID chip implant

I didn't even have to mention the fact that the shadows in power have been attempting to force Americans to inject RFID tracking devices under the skin for many years. Some suspect that this policy will be spawned from the ACA, as it will first be administered in order to help healthcare facilities immediately extract medical history with the convenient swipe of an RFID reading device.

Later on, these RFID tracking chips (yes, likened to the same that are already in many of our consumer goods) will be used to contain banking information, whereabouts, political affiliation, citizenship status, etc. If you are causing any kind of a problem for the powers-that-be, then they can simply turn off your chip.

Welcome to the twenty-first century. Now, fall in line and keep your head down.

At the end of the day, all of this power to track, trace, manipulate, and control will lie with the executive branch, the president of the United States of America. Basically, all the agencies and bureaucracies I mentioned in this chapter fall under White House control. From the Patriot Act under George W. Bush to the NDAA under Barack Hussein Obama, the executive branch has been successful in making the American people into enemies of the state, enemies who must be watched and manipulated at all costs. Through the IRS, NSA, CIA, DIA, EPA, etc., the U.S. government, in concert with the endless resources of the Oval Office, currently has the technological capacity to wreak havoc on the lives and liberties of the American people.

Nevertheless, this is not the time to live in fear, resorting to that blasted normalcy bias. No, burying our heads in the sand will not make the threat or the fear go away. Rather, simply ignoring the problem will only deepen it.

The common parable often told concerns a frog that is about to be boiled. If a frog is thrown directly into boiling water, then it will simply jump out of the pot. However, if that same frog is gently placed into cool water and the heat is slowly increased, the frog will be cooked before he knows it. If the frog had been aware of the cook's intentions all along, he would have recognized that he wasn't merely taking a warm bath in a stainless steel pot. The frog could simply jump out, continuing life and possibly freedom if he were quick and sly enough.

In the same way, all we need to do is jump towards our freedom. However, first, recognizing that we aren't simply taking a warm bath is the most essential step. I hope the first half of this book helped you understand this to be the case. The second step, which I will be discussing in the coming sections, is the act of jumping towards our freedom, out of the pot and away from the cook's grasp.

It is important to understand that the clock is ticking and has been for quite some time. Your life, liberty, and your pursuit of happiness is dependent on just how badly you desire to keep it. Sadly, it seems that our time for relying on the protections contained in the Constitution is coming to a close. We may soon have to rely on ourselves, the preparations we've made, our tenacity, our creativity, and our commitment to the ideals of ages past in order to keep us and our loved ones safe and free.

In the next section, we will go over the categories of information that you need to protect. This next section will aid in your understanding of what personal data that identity criminals want, as well as what information corporations and White House bureaucracies already have.

Having an accurate view of the very real threat to our privacy is half the battle of keeping our good names in the proper hands. The second half is preparing and executing the necessary measures to be able to move about without being seen. If hell is on the way, then perhaps we might be able to pass through without the devil knowing we were there in the first place.

SECTION THREE

What They Want From You

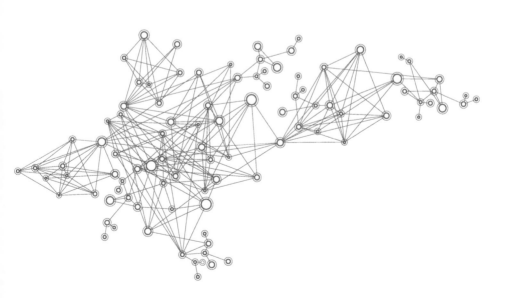

Chapter 10

NAMES AND NUMBERS: THE TARGET ON YOUR BACK

To live in the twenty-first century, it is important to understand the value of our numbers and documents that recognize our names. Our numbers are the designation that was given to us. We don't pick them in the same way a mother picks a name for a child. No, our numbers are assigned to us, so that we can be *easily identified* in the ever-flowing sea of humanity.

The fact that numbers provide a way for an individual to be identified quickly is also what makes them both a convenience and a liability. They are convenient in that we are not confused with others, and the numerical (or alphanumerical) value offers a much faster ability to locate a single account. However, they are also a liability, as it depends on *who* is using account numbers to find an individual. The one locating the individual may have malicious intent.

Numerical account systems are merely tools, which means they are not inherently good or evil. It is the character and intent of the entity using these systems that is what decides *why* these systems are being used. For instance, using an account number comes in handy when hoping to receive customer service. It becomes a problem when someone has gotten a hold of your numbers, intending to do you harm.

In addition, any time the government issues you a document or card that recognizes your name and place among the totality of the U.S. citizenry, it can also become a liability to you. These documents define us in the eyes of America's most powerful entities and if they are compromised, you will realize just how important they really were. From them, an identity thief can start a whole new existence, all the while destroying yours like a mind-altering virus.

In this chapter, we are going to go through numbers and documents that you need to protect, as they can be targets on your back if you aren't careful. It is important to think of these as defensive gates: they make a convenient way to get inside, but they also compose the weakest section in your wall. You must protect the gate at all costs.

SOCIAL SECURITY NUMBER

For U.S. citizens, your Social Security number is how the government identifies you. Without it, you cannot easily buy a car, open a bank account, file your taxes, find work, find a place to live, seek medical care, and a host of other things. Your Social Security number is your *most important number* for the simple fact that it is the key to accessing the most basic parts of civilized life in America.

This is the most prevalent reason why your SSN is your most coveted number in the identity theft world. With a stolen SSN, one has the capacity to become the victim in every sense. It is your broadest gate and the road going through it is an eight-lane highway.

If one were trying to assume a false identity, they must begin with a Social Security number. The SSN is the foundation to your identity as recognized by local, state, and federal governments. Without the SSN, you are an undocumented person, and since Uncle Sam has gained such powerful influence in almost every aspect of life, undocumented persons cannot have a standard of living much beyond a homeless panhandler. This is one reason why illegal immigrants will pay premium prices in order to acquire a stolen, clean Social Security number.

Because Social Security numbers have so many uses for an individual, identity thieves have struck gold when they successfully extract one.

HOW YOUR SOCIAL SECURITY NUMBER CAN BE USED

As we mentioned, Social Security numbers are the foundation, the most essential part of living under a different identity. Through merely acquiring an SSN, a fraudster can easily find employment and even a place to live. In addition, it is possible to receive government assistance, healthcare, and even cash by using a stolen SSN. Illegal immigrants have been using this method for decades.

In addition, one scam that appears to be growing in popularity is tax refund fraud. Someone, using a stolen SSN, can submit a fraudulent tax refund to the IRS and will then receive a large check in the mail weeks later. If the identity thief covered his or her tracks well enough, the only paper trail will go back to the victim of the theft.

While we did say that using the SSN is the foundation to assuming a second identity, it is only the beginning piece of the puzzle. The SSN is essential, but proficient identity thieves know that they need further documentation in order to be able to extract wealth and live under a second identity in order to throw the authorities off of their trail.

BIRTH CERTIFICATE

Your birth certificate is the U.S. government's way of saying they acknowledge that you exist. This means that it is perhaps your most important document. If your birth certificate becomes compromised, then someone else has compromised your own existence in the eyes of the U.S. government.

A birth certificate will allow an identity thief to become you, but it isn't the only document they will need. Keep in mind that a birth certificate on its own will not offer very much by way of capability. A birth certificate is almost useless if some other form of identification does not accompany it. However, if the identity thief has access to a Social Security number, a utility bill, or a life insurance policy, it is possible to literally assume the identity of the victim.

In summary, on its own, a birth certificate has little capacity for a fraudster to make use of a second identity. Accompanied with other easily acquired documentation, it is one of the most authenticating documents the thief could have stolen.

DRIVER'S LICENSE OR STATE ID CARD

Your driver's license or state ID card is perhaps your most used form of identification for both government and private functions. Obviously, a driver's license is necessary to have while operating a motor vehicle, but it is requested for employment applications, government benefits, and even when trying to buy tobacco products and alcohol if you appear to be a young person.

Alone, a driver's license will enable a fraudster to move about on a surface level, and it can even act as a free pass when stopped by police. If the driver's license is clean and suspicious activity has not been reported, police let the fraudster go. Essentially, it is seen as the first layer of protection for many proficient criminals trying to operate without using their real identities.

IDENTITY THEFT RULE OF 3S

As you can see, with only one form of identification, it is difficult for an identity thief to be able to operate effectively. However, if a thief has a two-piece combination of a victim's birth certificate, a social security number, or a driver's license, the thief can literally assume a full-blown second identity. This is the principle that we call the ID Theft Rule of 3s.

Also, in following this rule, two parts can easily construct the third. With only two of these three documents, the identity thief can officially acquire the third within thirty days.

For instance, if a thief has acquired a birth certificate and Social Security number, he or she has the capability of acquiring a driver's license. If the thief has a driver's license and a birth certificate, the thief can acquire a reprint of a Social Security card. With a Social Security number and a driver's license, the thief can acquire a birth certificate reprint.

Of course, this rule refers to general factors, as all this depends on a myriad of other aspects such as state and county laws, and the ability of the fraudster to follow protocol effectively. For instance, if the state has turned to biometric fingerprinting systems, the identity thief will probably try to operate from a state that does not.

In addition, most government and private institutions will also require a life insurance policy, utility bill, medical bill, or some other documentation for additional proof of identity. This is one reason why it often takes at least thirty days to fully construct the paperwork necessary to operate under the secondary identity. Of course, many of these documents are easily falsifiable. Oftentimes, it only requires the presentation of a Social Security number or a driver's license to rent an apartment or office, and utility companies usually require those two exact documents in order to open an account. So, within thirty days, the perpetrator will receive those bills in the mail, which can be used immediately to acquire the third essential piece.

U.S. PASSPORT

On the subject of U.S. passports, we will explore two aspects. First, a U.S. passport is incredibly useful to an identity thief. Second, a passport can be constructed by the ID Theft Rule of 3s.

A passport is seen as possibly the most authoritative form of identification because it requires a higher level of documentation to acquire one. This is why any employer, bank, credit agency, and even almost every government (provided the solvency of diplomatic relations, of course) will recognize a passport. In many cases, the provision of a passport will nullify the need to provide a secondary form of identification. For instance, in most cases, a driver's license and Social Security number is needed to begin employment, but some corporations and reputable businesses will not even require a copy of a Social Security card if a passport is presented.

Also, a passport (or passport renewal) can be acquired through an effectively constructed second identity. However, one reason why passports are considered as an authoritative document is because passports *require all three* forms of identification and the photo must closely match the appearance of the victim.

Thus, it is incredibly important to keep your passport secure. If you find your passport has been stolen or compromised in any way, call the U.S. Department of State *immediately*.

TOTAL ID THEFT

Total identity theft is what happens when a victim's complete identity is stolen and used for more than just financial gains. In effect, the perpetrator assumes the victim's identity for an extended period of time, rather than quickly stealing the victim's assets and dumping the personal information within hours of its extraction.

The identity-defining documents we mentioned above are the keys to the gate, the means by which almost all total identity thieves can achieve their goals. Essentially, only the most audacious and effective criminals attempt this type of crime, but the payoff enables them to operate within the U.S. with clean paperwork. Even if the police stopped them, those names and numbers would come back as valid. The whole point of using a second total identity is that it enables the criminal to cease being a person he or she does not want to be.

Whether it is running from a criminal record, a warrant for arrest, a criminal investigation, a non-existent citizenship, or even a past life of regret, the second identity offers the ability for the fraudster's previous name to simply evaporate.

When the system cannot find a name, it is almost impossible to find the owner of that name.

However, in most cases, if you are reading this book, there is a very small chance that your total identity will be compromised. Essentially, someone who is actively using his or her own identity will quickly discover the existence of the crime and act immediately. It takes quite a bit of work and/or funding in order to assume a second identity, and if the secondary identity is burned in a short time, then it will not be worth the investment for the thief. You are most likely not going to be a victim anytime soon. (I say again: *most likely*.)

These are the most common victims of total identity theft:

- An infant
- Someone who is deceased and not well known
- Someone who is unable to operate within society from a mental or physical disorder
- Someone who is homeless or impoverished

Essentially, a functioning member of society is not at a high level of risk due to the current level of activity on the individual's identity. Identity thieves constructing a total identity will use a rather dormant identity or one that will not be used for many years.

Because of this, it is important that you look after the identities of those who fit the above-mentioned category. If you are a new parent, caring for an elderly person, responsible for the wellbeing of someone who is afflicted with a physical or mental disorder, or caring for the homeless or impoverished, then it is important that you keep these documents safe and protected.

The most reported cases of total identity theft occur when a close relative or family friend perpetrates the act. This seems like a logical finding, given the higher level of access that a close personal associate would have.

However, this is not to say that professional identity thieves are not currently operating and building total second identities. Perhaps the reason why professional identity thieves make the headlines less often is because they are skilled at evading authorities, and police have a tough time tracking down an unknown variable player (not a close associate). A ghost is always difficult to catch.

In criminal circles, extracting identities is a business. Illegal immigrants are able to obtain these identities, as professionals sell them at a premium. How do we know this?

While the government refuses to publish data in regards to total identity theft and illegal immigration, there are other published studies indicating that this is the case. NBC News reports:

> *Based on actual numbers of identity theft complaints reported to the trade commission in 2006, states bordering Mexico led the nation in identity theft victims per population. Arizona ranked first—followed by Nevada, California, Texas and Florida.*

That data showed 246,035 identity theft victims nationwide who reported at least one type of identity theft to the FTC in 2006. Employment-related fraud comprised 14 percent of the complaints nationwide, and about 11 percent of those reported by Kansas victims.

Professional identity theft does exist, and its most lucrative market appears to be located along the U.S.-Mexican border.

However, regardless of what, who, how, and why total identity theft takes place, it is important that you closely guard the identities of those in your care. Lock the documentation in a safe and keep track of those who know the combination.

COMMON IDENTITY THEFT

Common identity theft is far simpler in *modus operandi,* motivation, intent, and it is logistically easier for criminals to perpetrate. This, of course, is why it is more…common.

Basically, common identity theft occurs when your account numbers (such as bank accounts, credit cards, health insurance policy numbers, etc.) become compromised for a brief time. As opposed to total identity theft, common identity theft occurs for purely financial motivations, and the duration is almost always relatively short from beginning to end. As we mentioned in previous chapters, usually a common identity thief will only use the information for about forty-eight hours.

This type of theft, however, poses a danger to almost anyone not actively involved in protecting his or her information. Because it is much simpler and easier to perpetrate, common identity theft is much harder to prevent. Below are the account types and numbers that are the most vulnerable.

CREDIT AND DEBIT CARD NUMBERS

In order to compromise your credit card and debit card information, the only data the thief would need is displayed on the card itself. This is the essential information they must have:

- Credit card number (displayed on the front)
- Name as shown on the card (displayed on the front)

- Expiration date (displayed on the front)
- Security code
    - o   For American Express, the security code is four digits (displayed on the front)
    - o   For Visa/MasterCard, the security code is three digits (displayed on the back)

Identity thieves who are able to extract this information can purchase products online, through the mail, or by phone. In addition, seasoned thieves can use your credit card information through fabricating a counterfeit card with a functioning magnetic strip. These cards enable the identity thief to purchase assets quickly for resale and can be purchased online for roughly $20,000. These machines are becoming more and more commonly used among identity thieves. Debit or check cards are not at a high risk for this method, as the thief must also have access to the victim's PIN (personal identification number).

Of course, credit card and debit card identity theft can occur if your cards are lost or stolen. This method can be easily prevented by keeping track of your cards and reporting the situation if you are unable to locate them.

CHECKING ACCOUNT INFORMATION

If you are not in the practice of shredding your bank statements and voided checks, then there is a good chance that an identity thief can siphon the funds from your bank account until it's dry. How?

There are several methods, but it all starts with the extraction of your checking account info. Then, an identity thief can:

- Create counterfeit checks using blank check stock
- Use the *check washing method,* whereby the thief uses chemicals to remove and then print new information on the check
- Infiltrate your bank account and add an extra account holder, then withdraw funds.

You should keep close tabs on all of your account information, such as:

- Names
- Addresses

- Phone numbers
- Birth dates
- Phone number on the account
- Account number
- Routing number
- PIN (personal identification number)
- Password (for online banking)

MEDICAL INSURANCE POLICY INFORMATION

A very common practice, which is mostly perpetrated by someone who is close to the victim, is insurance policy fraud. It is important to make sure that you protect your policy number, group number, BIN, and any other information on the card that is specific to your policy.

When medical benefit fraud occurs, usually the perpetrator will go to the doctor's office having memorized certain information:

- Name of policy holder
- Date of birth
- Address
- Family physician

The numbers that they would extract from the card are the following:

- Policy number
- Group number
- BIN (bank identification number—this tells the computer database at the pharmacy which insurance provider is to receive the claim for your prescription coverage. No actual banks are involved in the billing process.)
- Any other information specific to the policy (due to the wide variation of information on health insurance cards)

In addition, if the thief has, in fact, stolen the insurance card, they can even swipe it through a reader like a credit card without having to memorize any other info. In some cases, the thief may also need another form of ID, but this is usually not standard procedure for medical billing offices.

The outcome of medical insurance policy fraud is that the victim receives the bill for the care administered to the identity thief. This also goes for government medical benefits as well.

ONLINE ACCOUNT USERNAME AND PASSWORDS

Perhaps one of the most overlooked categories of information is with online accounts. These days, even credit card information is stored and remembered for the convenience of one-click purchasing, processing payments, and releasing of funds. However, convenience can come at a rather high price.

If your password and username information is extracted, an identity thief can access your account and change account information. The thief would most likely change the address, phone number, and email address information so that the victim would remain unaware of purchase notifications. Once the "ship to" address had been changed, the thief then one-click purchases goods. Immediately thereafter, the thief changes all the information back to the way it was, and the goods are then shipped to the identity thief's desired address (probably an address that is a vacant building, apartment, or home).

Most victims never realize what has happened until the thief is long gone, having absconded with goods purchased from the victim's remembered credit card information. This is another reason to keep a close watch on browsers and other computer programs that remember account and password information.

Certainly guard your username and password information, but also make sure that you are keeping watch over your computer. Unauthorized access to your computer (through theft, hacking, key-stroke tracking devices, etc.) could result in a massive information leak, especially if you've given permission to various programs to remember your information.

Computer and online-based crimes are becoming more and more common, as the civilized world turns to cyberspace. Information sharing, business transactions, and even transfers in currency are almost exclusively taking place over the Internet. This means that is has become more important than ever to keep your online information guarded, and avoid displaying too much of it. In the next chapter, we will be discussing the inherent identity theft dangers of social networking utilities.

When displaying your life for the world to see, understand that distinguishing friend from foe becomes impossible through the veil of a computer screen. Online smiles from your "friends" may actually mask opportunistic smirks from your foes.

Chapter 11

INDECENT EXPOSURE: THE DANGERS OF SOCIAL NETWORKING UTILITIES

With 1.15 billion (yes, billion with a "b") users across the spectrum of social networking, it seems rather difficult these days to conduct any kind of business or keep up with friendships and acquaintances without those social networking utilities like Facebook, Twitter, LinkedIn and a host of other applications. While there are many social philosophers out there who disagree with the basic premise of using such conveniences, we are not necessarily going to cover that aspect. Indeed, services such as Facebook may certainly be chipping away at society's psychological fabric, creating narcissists, degrading languages, and further isolating us from real social interaction, but these utilities *do* have their strengths.

In terms of marketing, ease of contact, and the ability to network quickly and effectively, these social networking utilities (SNUs) do have a place. They certainly have the capability of facilitating terrible things, but they can also facilitate great things as well. They are tools, but like any tool, they can be used, abused…and exploited.

The key is to keep SNUs in your control, while not allowing them to control you. In addition, it is important to understand just how much power they have for the exploitation of privacy…for both corporate data mining companies, and identity thieves.

Since we have already covered the corporate data mining and government privacy invasion aspect of social networking utilities, this chapter is meant to cover the more practical topic of identity theft.

FROM THE PREDATOR'S PERSPECTIVE

One reason why many people like using SNUs such as Facebook is because it offers them the opportunity to find friends and be found by them also. In addition, we also mentioned that many use Facebook as a marketing tool. In fact, it sometimes acts as *the prime marketing tool* for many small businesses. Facebook is powerful in that it is a database of people, offering a way to look them up, and for corporate data mining companies to use the information extracted from each profile for marketing research.

In a database of 1.15 billion people, there is an extremely high chance that a person you are trying to find will have a profile or know someone who does. This would be a wonderful thing *if the world had no predators*. But unfortunately, there are many and they are getting very good at what they do.

Perhaps we should look at Facebook from a predator's perspective? His name is Frank Abagnale, the man who was one of the world's greatest con artists, and was also played by Leonardo DiCaprio in the movie *Catch Me If You Can*. He now works as one of the world's leading security consultants, which was quite the change from his former life where he had assumed a total of eight different identities over a span of several years. *Reuter's* reports on what Abagnale says is a real security risk on the part of folks who use Facebook:

> *If you tell me your date of birth and where you're born [on Facebook], I'm 98 percent [of the way] to stealing your identity," he said at an Advertising Week Europe conference on Wednesday. "Never state your date of birth and where you were born [on personal profiles], otherwise you are saying 'come and steal my identity.'"*

The report continues, stating Abagnale's advice to folks using SNUs and other services associated with possible privacy concerns:

> *He urges users to be careful about what they fill out and to make smart decisions—because ultimately, people can control what they put on the web.*

> *"Your privacy is the only thing you have left," he said. "Don't blame all the other companies—Google, Facebook—you control it. You have to keep control of your own information."*

This is certainly sound advice, especially considering the source. Coming from one who was a more-than-competent predatory identity thief, these words should be recorded, rewritten, and read over and over again. Yes, ladies and gentleman, you have to keep control of *your own* information and to add to this statement, the information of those for whom you are responsible.

According to Abagnale, SNUs have the potential to pose a serious information security risk. Not only does one have very little control over who can see a person's information, but also the information that is often posted can largely compose a full identity.

Even so, a predator can accomplish an identity heist without evening being anywhere near or knowing the victim. From behind a computer screen, the newest group of thieves no longer have to wear a mask.

In addition, an identity thief *could be anyone.* Just because a profile might appear to be a friend of yours doesn't mean that the individual is, in fact, someone you know. It is incredibly easy to be an imposter with the ability to copy and paste a picture and a name.

THE OPERATOR'S MODUS OPERANDI

Because of the comprehensive nature of Facebook profiles, that particular SNU has become perhaps one of the most dangerous. Let us consider what folks are posting on their profiles:

- Full name
- Date of birth
- Hometown
- Current town
- Pictures
- Pictures of family, friends, and associates
- Tagged pictures, identifying associates in pictures
- Time and location of pictures taken
- Place of business
- Work experience history
- Education history (preschool – higher education)
- Dates associated with work and education history transitions
- Real-time locations including mapping
- Activities listed in real-time (status posts)
- Church name and location

- Various organizations
- Various interests
- Various belief systems

…and the list could go on.

Years ago, this information could only be extracted through word-of-mouth, and associates would simply reply to the predator, "Who's asking?"

Now, the only filter is your ability to select the option of whether or not the general public can see this information or only known associates and friends. Then again, how many folks *actually* filter their friend requests. It's not always a difficult matter to become a friend of someone whom you have never met.

It is extremely easy to extract invaluable information from a person's profile through simply friending them. However, this isn't the only scam a Facebook predator can use.

THE WEB IS WOVEN

Though Facebook has labored to identify and delete multiple and false profiles, they most certainly *have not* tried hard enough. Some of the most active Facebook scammers have the ability to create false profiles, and also entire *networks* of false profiles in order to make the original impostor appear to be a *real person* who has friends. In this way, a person can hide behind the fabrication of alter-entities.

One practice is called *Facebook cloning*. This happens when an individual creates an entirely false profile of someone who already exists. When the victim accepts the friend request, they have no idea that the person in control of the false profile that sent the friend request is not actually the victim's friend. Again, just because you know someone who is on Facebook doesn't mean you actually *know* him or her.

Usually, cloning results in either the impostor getting a hold of information that the victim has already posted, or the clone will begin asking the victim questions.

This brings us to another cardinal rule of interacting with associates on Facebook, SNU, or another chat program:

How do you know that you are chatting with someone you know?

*Never give out your personal information, even if a friend or family member has asked for it, unless you can **hear the other person's voice or see the other person's face.***

In fact, the person you may be talking to in a chat session…might not even be a person at all.

One very common practice among SNU predators is to create non-entities called *bots*. Bots are programs that are designed to extract information from very large groups of people. These programs are actually quite easy to identify.

If you unknowingly friend a bot or add one to your contacts, you will notice that the other profile wants to chat immediately. During the chat, you will then notice that the bot seems to write painfully generic information, looping responses, almost as if the entire conversation was planned in advance. That is because *it was programmed that way.*

Essentially, the purpose of the bot will usually have two main objectives. First, the bot will immediately scour the information in your profile, or (and) it will try to extract information from you in the chat process. Sometimes, programmers can make their bots very convincing, giving varying responses, even timing a conversation to say something like "r u there?" after a small period of conversational silence.

In most cases, bots will be distributed far and wide, because most people can spot them pretty quickly. However, there are some who can be fooled by bots, pinpointing the perfect victims for the heist. Bot distribution is a numbers game: the more people the programmer can contact, the higher the chances of extracting valuable information from an unwitting victim.

Sometimes bots can be used for less nefarious purposes, of course. In some cases, it can be used as an unethical marketing practice, in which the bot will ask for the victim to join a membership or buy some kind of product. Or bots are utilized for the pure enjoyment of a simple hacker who's looking to get his or her kicks.

One of the most common scams that good folks have had to endure comes in the form of the predators copycatting *their victim's profile*. Essentially, the scam goes as follows:

- The con creates an alter profile of your valid one.

- He or she begins contacting your friends, family, and known associates, telling them of a heartbreaking tragedy in your life. Usually the tragedy will involve some kind of medical or travel expense.

- Then, the con requests funding, giving them a foreign address or bank account to which they should send the cash. (This scam usually originates overseas due to the inability for U.S. law enforcement to locate and prosecute the perpetrator or group of perpetrators.)

- The con receives the cash and laughs all the way to the bank, leaving your family and friends none the wiser and your credibility in shambles.

Nevertheless, how falsified profiles are used do not necessarily matter in terms of how you should conduct yourself on SNUs and other online services:

1. You should never post anything online that you wouldn't want your worst enemies and society's worst predators to know.

2. You should never accept a contact or friend request from someone you do not know.

3. You should never share any information unless you can see the other person's face or *hear* his or her voice.

MALEVOLENT COPY CATS, OVERSEAS LOVERS, AND THAT NO-NAME ORGANIZATION WHO HELPS POOR STARVING CHILDREN FROM...WHEREVER

Unfortunately, con artists are well aware that human affections and passions can have a rather favorable (or unfavorable, from your perspective) effect on your ability to identify a scam.

Two such scams come to mind:

- No-Name Organization
- Online Dating Scam

It is not uncommon to find non-profit organizations on Facebook. In fact, Facebook is perhaps one of their best ways to connect with prospective supporters. However, this is a golden opportunity for the dirtiest of scammers.

If you are ever hit up on Facebook by some random individual or a cloned friend, asking for support of the No-Name Organization, then be sure to do your homework before sending the check. Of course, there are certainly reputable and good organizations that are legitimately doing philanthropic work, so be sure to say something along the lines of "Let me do some research, and I'll get back to you if I can offer support." If your background research doesn't check out, then call the authorities immediately, and they will get to the bottom of the situation.

Indeed, love for humanity is not the only kind of passion that has been known to swindle unwitting victims out of their dollars. For instance, the online dating world (another SNU that is often overlooked) is certainly ripe for scams, especially since emotions of hopeful romance have a way of clouding judgment. They prey on the loneliness and good intentions of their target:

- Attractive "lady" (probably using a false picture) contacts the profile of an unwitting man.

- Lady lives overseas (but, of course), and either claims she is in a bad situation requiring the generous donation of funds, or the only way to get her to America is by the victim funding the trip.

- Unwitting man takes the bait, and wires or mails the funds overseas, never to hear from the "lady" again.

Indeed, it is always important to never give information or especially send money without proper verification in place. If you don't know them, then this is even more crucial.

However, some predators aren't even after money. Unfortunately, they simply wish to see your world burn. Why? It is the symptom of a vendetta against you, their target. To predators such as these (the most malevolent among them), SNUs such as Facebook are often a prime weapon of mass destruction.

One of the biggest reasons why it is important to never post any information you would not entrust to your *bitterest enemies* (whether you think you have any or not) is because posting that information publically on Facebook is basically doing just that.

Especially if you are some kind of leader or person of authority, or someone with money, power, or influence, then there is a chance you may have enemies and may not even know it. Real enemies will not attack from the light, but approach from behind, from the shadows. They lurk in the dark, they will never reveal their true agenda, and they mean to do you harm, *even at their own cost.*

Enemies aren't always concerned with making a buck, but are operating for the purpose of inflicting damage. In some cases, the objective is purely self-gratifying. In other cases, the objective is more sophisticated, mounting the attack for political, personal, legal, financial, or social gain. Nevertheless, SNUs have a way of being very useful for those who wish to do harm to others, using these tools as a way to unethically defeat their adversaries.

For instance, cloning can also be used to assassinate your character. The predator can actually create a profile and make your friends, associates, employees, constituency, or whoever, think that it *is you.* The only difference between this attack and the cloning scam we mentioned above is the fact that the end objective is more malevolent than financially motivated.

Once folks have taken the bait, the predator can rip your character asunder, tearing it limb from limb through doctored or personal photos, offensive posts, or whatever else will destroy your reputation. Blackmail is another possibility with this particular scenario.

THE IMPORTANCE OF GOOD PASSWORDS

Overall, no information is more important for the security of your SNU profiles than your login information. Because you username will be easy to access and widely known, it is crucial that you have a very strong password and change it often. Especially with an SNU like Facebook, this is extremely important in light of what we've been discussing.

Why?

Imagine if an enemy were able to get a hold of your password. Not only would he or she be able to destroy your reputation via access to a profile that your Facebook friends *know* to be yours, but also the predator can lock you out by changing the security information. In that event, it could take a while to fix the situation, since you would have to contact Facebook directly, and *they* would have to retake the account. At that point, the damage has been done, as the changes would have been broadcasted all over the newsfeed. In twenty-four hours, your social life could take damage that might require years to repair.

In addition, the same type of scam is possible, especially if the victim is able to contact your friends, family, and associates asking for money. Coming directly from your own profile, a sob story would be infinitely more convincing. The financial damage done to your family and friends could be extensive, and your credibility and reputation would be adversely affected.

DON'T DROP YOUR GUARD, ESPECIALLY ONLINE

Frank Abagnale certainly had a point. You are truly responsible for the security of your own information. We cannot blame Facebook or any SNU for our unwillingness to take identity theft and privacy concerns seriously. You do not have to post potentially dangerous personal information on these SNUs, and you do so at your own risk. In addition, you *do not have to* trust someone just because they are your contact or your Facebook friend.

Keeping this in mind, understand that it requires a change in perspective in order to fully understand the nature of information security. Rather than regarding everyone you meet online as a friend, it is perhaps best to regard them as a potential liability. It is only when you *hear a voice and see a face* that you should trust the other individual. This makes sense, considering the inherent nature of the online SNU minefield.

Also, as we learned from cloning and password hacking scams and attacks, your family and friends depend on your ability to secure your information and keep a level head when interacting with folks online.

Online, trust no one: the good people in your life depend on it.

Chapter 12

THE PREDATORS GO MOBILE

We have explored the inherent dangers of identity theft and privacy issues that originate from your basic information and social networking utilities. To most privacy-conscious folks, these are obvious areas to guard. However, there are still other areas that require special attention, as the predators are always evolving (often faster than our attempts to thwart them).

The advent of the smartphone has opened a Pandora's box of avenues, which the predators can use to extract your valuable information, even possessing the ability to usurp control of your mobile devices. This has the possibility of becoming a frightening situation as time and technology march forward.

Especially in American society, the smartphone is quickly and fundamentally changing the way an individual interacts with the world. In a philosophical sense, mobile devices are becoming an individual's perpetual umbilical cord to this hyper-connected society, especially considering how almost all social interaction and business dealings are being consolidated into this technology. To illustrate this, watch what happens when an average Joe loses or breaks his smartphone. Panic, disconnect, damage in productivity, paranoia, and all kinds of mental drug-withdrawal-like symptoms take hold.

In support of this claim, it seems as if smartphone saturation has crossed a threshold. *Forbes.com* reports:

> *Two separate surveys confirmed that smartphone penetration has not only passed half of all mobile subscribers, but has gone well beyond 50 percent of all adult Americans for the first time.*

Because a smartphone is an all-encompassing technological device, which stores vast amounts of information and connects the individual to several integral networks, it is perhaps a safe assumption that over 50% of Americans are attached to society through this technological umbilical cord (at least according to the Forbes report on those surveys).

Understanding this societal smartphone dependency, it is no wonder why identity thieves are evolving to meet these newest golden opportunities. Folks store mountains of personal information from passwords to pictures on their smartphones and mobile devices. Opportunistic predators will not want to waste any time in exploiting them.

However, are there really *that many methods* for an identity thief to extract and exploit your information from a smartphone?

Unfortunately, the predators have been busy. They already have quite a few methods at their disposal, and security tech seems to have faltered in the escalation race. The predators are already on the prowl, and our attempts to repel them are still in their infancy.

OVERSEAS TECH INVASION

Perhaps the most unnerving aspect about hackers, con artists, and identity thieves who using smartphones to exploit personal information is the fact that the tech is becoming cheaper and easier to use.

Unfortunately, many Americans often find themselves in a mind-bubble of sorts, not understanding that just because a product is illegal in America, doesn't mean it is illegal in other countries.

For some reason, China comes to mind when in considering this principle.

In fact, identity thieves and hackers are big fans of China's relaxed property policies, using the products and software that originate from that country on a regular basis. We know that some of the best fake IDs, hacker software, pirated entertainment media, and especially illegal electronic devices are openly sold and easily acquired through the Chinese market.

But of course, China is not the only concern. Perhaps the reason why China is such a priority concern for tech security is because it is one of the only economies on the planet that is advanced enough to produce such high-tech devices and software, while at the same time, is one that seems devoid of common-sense property protection laws.

YOUR INFORMATION: THEIR GOLD MINE

Bear in mind that most smartphone and mobile device hackers will usually attack for a very simple reason—because they can. However, if you are in a position of importance, influence, or you've simply landed on the hit list of an identity thief that is in business for obvious financial gain, then things are about to get very creepy, *very quickly.*

Because smartphones are so…*smart,* they provide a comprehensive, extensive picture into who you are, where you go, whom you know, what you're doing, and when you're doing it. These devices can perform this to an extent that corporate data mining companies can only dream of accomplishing. Why? The reason is rooted in the illusion of near-total privacy. When you think you are being watched or followed, you act differently, shielding yourself against the watcher(s) to protect your vulnerabilities. However, when you are unaware and have a false sense of security, then you will simply divulge your vulnerabilities without a second thought.

This relaxed psychological state, which is driving identity thieves towards the practice of going after smartphones and mobile devices, is perhaps the most obvious motivator for the increasing rate at which smartphone identity thieves are attacking.

Knowing this, identity thieves want (and will potentially have access to) the following personal data and will possess these capabilities:

- Full name
- Smartphone password information
- Phone number on the device and account
- Usage history
- Your present and real-time location
- Mobile provider subscription information
    - o   Credit card information (associated with the account)
    - o   Account holder information (full name, address, account number)
    - o   Type of account (services, lines, devices, etc.)
    - o   Date of birth listed on account
    - o   Social Security number
    - o   Any other verification or account information that is requested by mobile provider

- Apps used
  - o Credit card information (associated with the app)
  - o Mobile banking information (depending if mobile banking is being used)
  - o Games used
  - o Tools used

- Basic functions
  - o Picture history
  - o Message history
  - o Email history
  - o Control of your email accounts connected with the phone
  - o Control of the camera
  - o Control of the microphone
  - o Control of SMS
  - o Control of calling and receiving calls
  - o Control of your browser
  - o Control of your apps
  - o Control of your social networking utility apps

- Syncing
  - o Access to your other syncing devices (computers, printers, etc.)
  - o Access to your inbox program
  - o Access to your cloud
  - o Access to your entertainment
  - o Access to your contacts
  - o Access to your hard drive information after syncing

If an identity thief is able to gain unfettered access to your smartphone and mobile devices, they can literally take over your entire social, financial, and private life. Whereas some thieves will work quite hard to gain this kind of access by hijacking SNUs or other accounts, access to a person's smartphone has the potential to be absolutely devastating.

Not only could your financial information become totally compromised, but also from the information that can be gained through your mobile device, you could be subject to blackmail tactics. In a nightmare scenario, not only could the thief drain your accounts dry, but the thief could also cover his or her tracks by threatening the release of your private, most intimate information *if you were to attempt to contact the authorities.*

Your smartphone may be more important than you might have originally considered—both to you and to the hackers. Historically, there has never been such a wide gate of access to someone's identity without ever meeting the individual face-to-face.

To illustrate this point, Parmy Olson of *Forbes.com* discusses how hackers were able to use smartphone hacking techniques in order to listen in on a board meeting. The result was a massive transfer of wealth:

> *The crackers had set up a false, rogue cell tower in the near vicinity, and surreptitiously turned on his device's mic once the company meeting was underway. Not long after, an organization shorted the stock of his firm and netted themselves $30 million. The incident took place in the last year, according to Gregg Smith, the CEO of mobile security company KoolSpan, and is by no means an isolated case. In fact, researchers say it's becoming easier to take control of certain Android device features, like the mic or camera, with free online tools that are becoming more user friendly.*

The ability to hijack a smartphone is a truly powerful tool in the hacker's arsenal, and when used effectively, it can result in catastrophic damages to the victim, and in this case, $30 million in profits for the perpetrators.

STUDYING THE PREDATOR

As the *Forbes* article stated, hackers are able to acquire many of the tools necessary to accomplish their goals "with free online tools that are becoming more user friendly." This means, whereas once high costs and low availability of tools prevented the numbers of cons, hackers, and identity thieves from growing, this is no longer the case. High availability and low cost of tools, in addition to the relatively easy nature of the methods involved, are resulting in rapidly growing numbers of new identity thieves. Opportunity has knocked and they are answering.

As we mentioned before, the wide availability of Chinese tech, software, and devices are a major cause of the problem. IEEE.org discusses how powerful this can be in the hands of even the most inexperienced of hackers:

> *According to the* Times, *Alperovitch, along with a team of other security specialists, started with Nickispy (a Trojan Horse remote access tool emanating from China that disguised itself as a Google+ app), reversed engineered it, and then were able to successfully get the malware to load on an Android-based smartphone through a self-created phishing email. Once loaded, the smartphone functions, including all voice communications, could be completely accessed by a malicious remote user. Alperovitch also says once loaded, "there is no security software that would thwart it."*

Essentially, a hacker can literally take control of a smartphone or mobile device through loading an easily acquired Chinese-originated malware Trojan via a phishing email or message.

In addition, the article states that the program can be bought online for $300-$540. To someone who has the potential to extract thousands of dollars from unwitting victims, it is well worth the investment. In fact, the worst part is the fact that "there is no security software that would thwart it."

After scouring report after report of identity theft that takes place through smartphones, it is becoming rather apparent that the more sophisticated the device, scheme, or software, the easier it is to slip in and take control of the smartphone. The less sophisticated the scheme, the more the owner of the device has the ability of simply denying access.

In the same *Forbes* article we mentioned above, Olson talks about a certain program, like Nickispy, which hackers are using to gain access to smartphones:

AndroRAT can retrieve a phone's call logs, monitor SMS messages and calls, take photos and make a call. Once a would-be cracker has downloaded the remote access tool, they can use the binder to package AndroRAT into a legitimate-looking app, such as a game like Angry Birds. The binder costs $37 to buy online, while AndroRAT is free and open source.

Again, had the user simply refused to download the legitimate-looking app, then AndroRAT would never have been able to commandeer the smartphone.

OTHER WAYS THEY MAKE IT WORTH THEIR WHILE

The value of information, as we've discussed, is always rising. Since one can do so much with someone else's good name, it pays for an identity thief to basically acquire information to sell.

However, it is not uncommon for many of these viruses to hijack a phone, purchase and use apps, and send premium SMSs that the identity thief already controls. The result is that the hacker laughs all the way to the bank at the victim's expense. For instance, Parmy Olson's *Forbes.com* article states,

Sometimes attackers will just want to steal contact information, which depending on its origins can be highly prized in underground markets. Other times they'll want the hijacked phone to send premium SMSs. In the latter case, victims can remain oblivious until they see the extra digits on their monthly bill—Trojaned apps can also intercept warnings messages from carriers and delete them.

OTHER SIMILAR METHODS USED

In addition to the ability to hack just smartphones, laptops (and any other device that utilizes coffee shop-style Wi-Fi) are subject to potential attacks.

For instance, there are always new, cheap, or free plug-ins available to perform this function. For those of us who use Firefox to browse the web on our laptops, especially when we are connected to free Wi-Fi, there is a program that is designated as a *packet sniffer*. The program is called Firesheep.

Firesheep is a plug-in that can be loaded onto the Firefox browser and when it is in, it can intercept the cookies of other folks who are simultaneously using the Wi-Fi network. In layman's terms, the person using Firesheep has the ability to see your browser history and (possibly) login information, as these are almost always loaded onto our cookies. For instance, if you were using Amazon.com at the time a person in the same network was using Firesheep, they now have the ability to hack into your account.

Interestingly enough, Firefox has attempted to blacklist this plug-in, but even if they did, it would not matter. A Firefox browser can still disable the blacklist and download the program.

In addition, there has also been a plug-in that was recently released that uses the same exact modus operandi, but it's for the Android smartphone platform.

WORDS OF ADVICE

At the end of the day, we still largely have a choice to *refuse* to be a victim. While there are many highly sophisticated methods that can infiltrate our mobile devices, the vast majority of identity thieves are going to be using the methods we mentioned above.

These methods, as deceptively diabolical as they seem, still require the victim to choose *not to* diligently protect his or her devices. Parmy Olson of *Forbes* gives sound words of advice:

> *"Make sure the app, when installing, is only requesting permissions on the phone for what it intends to do," he says. "If the calculator is asking to read your e-mail, there's probably something wrong there."*

Essentially, you have to decide to download and open an app of unknown origin, *you* have to decide to take the bait from a phishing email, and *you* have to decide to use unprotected Wi-Fi.

If something seems phishy, off, or *just not right,* don't take the bait. Living by that policy can keep you and your devices out of a great deal of trouble.

Chapter 13

YOUR MISCELLANEOUS INFO: LOOSE ENDS TO TRIM

We've covered a good many aspects about what the predators are after. Keeping an eye on the weak points in your information wall will help you stave off disaster when you come into contact with a possible predator.

Indeed, there are certainly highly accomplished hackers, cons, and identity thieves and when they hit, you will have no idea from where the attack originated. While we may not necessarily be able to keep out every single threat, looking like a harder target to hit will limit your overall chances of having to deal with identity theft. However, this sort of problem is usually considered a statistical anomaly, (sort of like winning big bucks from scratch lottery tickets). The simple principle of reducing your profile and appearing like a much harder target tends to keep the thieves away.

Since most identity thieves are on the prowl for financial gain, it makes little sense to strike harder targets when there are endless opportunities for much softer targets. For the financially motivated thieves, they take the principles of risk, time, energy, and resources into account. If a target has reduced his or her vulnerabilities to the point where the risk, time, energy, and resources cost more than the value of succeeding, the con will simply not attack and will move on to a different, easier target.

You may not be invincible to identity theft, but you don't have to be. We will delve deeper into these principles in the next section. Nevertheless, the reason why we decided to touch on this point is because it may be financially or logistically difficult for you to tie off all of your loose ends. The basic reason why we are highlighting the possible weaknesses and talking about what they want is so that you are simply aware of your risks.

Awareness is the prelude to preparedness, and the more you know, the more you will be able to understand what protections are feasible in your life and which ones are not. The rest is up to you.

In this chapter, we will briefly discuss the possible miscellaneous vulnerabilities that can be exploited if left unprotected. Most identity thieves, hackers, and cons will run repeatable schemes that they learned from other thieves, hackers, and cons. Those types of schemes are the most common and occur on a statistically regular basis. However, every once in a while, there are thieves that come up with rather original ideas. They don't learn from anyone, but craft their own schemes that are based on their own research and intelligence.

The goal of this chapter is to enlighten you to the identity theft that could come out of left field. In doing so, this helps you understand what the predators want and gives you original perspective on how to achieve the invisibility objective that we will discuss in the next section.

CHEESE PIZZA WITH A SIDE OF IDENTITY THEFT

One of the most common places from which identity theft epidemically originates is from the food business. However, there is one particular type of food business that is particularly susceptible: delivery services.

Of course, there are many types of business that deliver to the home. However, food delivery is often a breeding ground for identity theft issues due to the frequency, circumstances, and relaxed security measures that are common in this industry. For instance, the Atlanta Journal-Constitution reported on a case in August of 2010:

When she realized her credit card was being used by someone on the other side of the country, a California woman called police in Georgia.

Since the stolen credit card number was being used to order pizza and pay electric bills, it didn't take long for Villa Rica police to crack the case, Capt. Keith Shaddix told the AJC.

"If you order pizzas online or on the phone, they deliver it your house," Shaddix said.

Essentially, the scam goes as follows:

The customer calls the pizza place and orders using a credit card. The order is made, and the delivery driver sets out to the location of the customer.

One of the most common practices that food delivery companies use is to take a crayon and rub the receipt over the customer's credit card, essentially copying the entire credit card number, expiration date, and full name on the card.

Food delivery businesses do this to make sure that you aren't scamming them. However, the reverse is most likely about to occur. Even so, sometimes the delivery driver is also the person you spoke with over the phone. They could have been copying down your info during the call, which is another common problem.

Where the driver was able to extract the security number on the back is by fidgeting, turning over the card, and simply remembering the three-digit code.

Then, on the way back to the shop, the driver pulls over, copies the information, adds in the security code from their memory. At this point, they literally have everything he or she needs in order to sap every last penny from the credit limit or debit account.

Many identity theft studies have suggested that sit-down restaurants are at the highest risk for this sort of scheme. However, we believe that this only appears to be the case because there are far more sit-down transactions than delivery transactions on a regular basis.

The food delivery business is one of the few where a lone employee is able to have extended and unsupervised access to essential credit card information, in addition to the victim's address and security code. Basically, the driver has it all, and they would be virtually impossible to catch in the act.

To answer the question of what they want from you is easy:

- Credit card information

- Full information on front (full name, credit card number, and expiration date)

- Security code on back

- Full address of the victim

The solution to this issue is rather simple. First, it is always best to pay with a cash transaction, especially with food delivery. Next, don't support restaurants that use the antiquated method of securing payment by rubbing the receipt with a crayon, as there are just too many security issues associated with it. Ask if they do before you make the transaction, and if they do, then politely stop the transaction and use their local competition that doesn't.

If this isn't feasible, then be sure to pay for the order using a credit card that has a different address on the account and not the address to which the driver is delivering. Since most off-site credit card transactions require a billing address, it makes it more difficult for the identity thief to use your information.

Be sure to watch the delivery driver when he or she is handling your credit card. If he or she fidgets, drops the card, or somehow suspiciously turns over the card for a few seconds, then you should assume that he or she is attempting to memorize the security code. In the event that this happens, politely ask, "Do you need the security code?" This sounds like an innocent, non-accusatory question. However, a driver that is actually attempting identity theft will interpret this as cause for aborting the scam, as they've been caught looking. He or she will most likely call it a night or simply move to another victim.

If the delivery person really gave you strong signals …then give the restaurant a non-threatening call. Simply say, "I just wanted to let you know that the delivery driver that was sent to my home seemed a little eager to see the security code on my card." This will both cover you in the event that identity theft actually occurs, and it may even lead to an investigation of their employee. Of course, you're not going on a witch-hunt. You're just tipping off the restaurant to the possibility of identity theft.

GENEALOGY REQUEST SCAM

As we have previously stated, it is important to understand where your biggest information leaks will occur. In addition, the ability to identify scams is crucial, especially when a certain establishment looks otherwise legitimate.

For instance, the curiosity about our ancestors has given way to a massive industry of genealogy investigators. It is rather easy to find online companies that can lead a person to finding out about his or her ancestry. It gives us a wonderful sense of importance, especially when we find out about the great things our ancestors accomplished.

However, this is one instance when you will need to do a fair amount of digging and homework on the genealogy research company you decide to use. Using the wrong company, or one where their informational security procedures are severely lacking, could give way to a hemorrhaging of personal information into the wrong hands.

One of the most common security measures that businesses use is to request names of family members and past associations.

Very clever identity thieves have recently been setting up small genealogy research operations because they know that their customers will simply hand over this information.

Perhaps the most effective part about the scam itself is the fact that the predators have intentionally maneuvered themselves into a place of trust with their intended targets. If they ask for personal data, they are usually going to get it, as it helps with their "research."

Overall, there are three ways to ensure that this unfortunate situation doesn't happen to you:

- First, only use businesses that have been well established, known nationally, and already have good reviews. While new genealogy research companies may advertise a cost savings and personal service, you may take an unnecessary risk using them.

- Second, if you do find a genealogy research company or very small operation, be sure that you do an extensive amount of homework on the employees and security practices of the company. Perhaps one of the best rules to follow is to only work with the company if you meet those running it face to face. Most identity thieves want nothing to do with a face-to-face meeting with a target.

- Last, keep tabs on the information you hand over. Some of this information is highly sensitive, especially considering the fact that it can be used to access online accounts. If you do have to give over information that seems irrelevant to the company's research efforts, then you may want to begin asking questions in regards to why they need it.

Asking a lot of questions is a surefire way to deter the con artists. Predators may even see you as a threat, because the more information you have, the easier it is for law enforcement to track them down after the fact. They would rather prey upon easy, unaware, and naive targets, as they present the lowest risk with the highest reward.

FALSE EMPLOYMENT OPPORTUNITIES

The employment opportunity scam is perhaps even more dangerous than the genealogy research scam. Because the unemployment rate has been high since 2008, people are less picky about which jobs they take. Thus, if a particular job seems too good to be true, or they seem to be asking for too much personal information, they may still snag quite a few people.

In addition, false employers are in a position where they can extract all the necessary information in order to wreak havoc on the job applicants. For instance, a false employer will have access to the following information:

- Full name

- Address

- Date of birth

- Social Security number

- Previous employment history

- Bank account and routing information

They would also be in possession of copies of your driver's license information, as well as your Social Security card or even your U.S. passport. With this information, the predators would easily be able to open accounts in your name.

Just like the genealogy request scam, with the false employment scam, the identity thieves would run the operation and then make their exit. In many cases, the police go to find the perpetrators after tracking down the address of the office from which they were working, only to happen upon an empty work space.

Identity thieves realize that, if they linger in the same place too long, it increases their chances of being caught. Thus, only ambiguous information is used and after the investigation begins, they are long gone.

Chapter 14

THE OVERSEAS THREAT

The world has never been smaller and because of that, identity theft threats can attack us from halfway around the world. Because of overseas outsourcing and the Internet, our information can fly to any corner of the globe, and unfortunately this is very difficult to prevent.

Perhaps the biggest reason why many of these issues originate from third world countries is due to the lack of laws and effective law enforcement. It is much easier to pull off identity theft from Pakistan rather than Pennsylvania for the following reasons:

- First, there are too few property and privacy laws to effectively prosecute these threats.

- Second, because law enforcement is already inadequate, it is much easier for the predators to get away with identity theft, even if there are laws in place.

- Third, if the crimes take place in another nation, but affect U.S. citizens in America, it is much more difficult for the U.S. to bring the perpetrators to justice.

- Fourth, if the attacks originate from overseas, the perpetrators are much harder to track down due to the change in basic infrastructure, laws, etc.

These are some of the reasons why many overseas scams that make the headlines are entire operations of well-organized con artists. In the U.S., this is logistically difficult to pull off, but from third world countries, they can easily fly under the radar.

In addition, the "lone wolf" identity thief is as much of a threat overseas, especially considering the relaxed privacy policies adopted by foreign firms. In many cases, these firms will have access to your tax, medical, and financial information, and unfortunately, if an identity theft takes place as a result from one of these companies, it is very difficult to find the perpetrator. The trend also appears to be growing. Antone Gonsales of InformationWeek.com writes:

Increasingly, however, companies with facilities overseas are contracting with U.S. hospitals, accounting firms, and insurance companies. The services these outsourcers provide include tax preparation, processing of insurance and medical claims, and transcribing dictation from doctors relating to all areas of the health-care process, from patient visits to surgical procedures.

Essentially, overseas firms possess much more information than they used to, which makes it very easy for someone to exploit your information. Because there is a big chance that they would never be caught and prosecuted, the usual deterrents are no longer an obstacle, and the statistical risks of overseas identity theft are rising faster.

THE LONE WOLVES

Overseas, a lone wolf can be a hundred times more dangerous than in the U.S. for the simple fact that it would be very easy for him or her to slip through the cracks. In addition, because an overseas firm may not have the same level of confidentiality with private information, this becomes a breeding ground for identity thieves.

Essentially, lone wolf thieves operate through U.S.-paid firms. These firms are usually English-speaking call centers, as many U.S. companies are outsourcing this kind of service. In many cases, these call centers will have the same information, especially billing information, that the corporate offices do in the U.S. This means that if you are using a U.S. firm that handles your business taxes or your books for your home business, this call center overseas has access to the innermost workings of your business. Because there may be an operating identity thief in the call center, your entire business is potentially at risk.

In addition, the black market for this information is very active in the third world. Identity theft weighs nothing, carries no inventory requirement, can be put into practice with very little investment, and results in the acquisition of U.S. dollars. This becomes extremely valuable in poor countries. It would be very easy for a lone wolf to extract this information, then resell it on the black market. It could take decades for this scam to catch up to the identity thief, and by that time, the thief is already long gone.

THE MACHINE

The instances where the most damage is done happens when entire groups of identity thieves conspire and create an overseas "company." Of course, the true nature of the company is not revealed, but these types of operations usually come in the form of employment opportunities.

Almost the exact method is used by domestic identity thieves except, because it exists overseas, the false employment scam model is thrown into overdrive. These companies usually claim that their business is a "work-from-home" opportunity, or follow along the lines of "make money online" schemes. However, what really happens is that you give over all your information, the predators package it up, and they sell the information to the highest bidder. These scams can go on for years, evading detection.

Because consumer protection laws are not in place, one very common issue is that these "companies" will require an upfront fee. Not only are they able to walk away with your confidential employment information, but they will also make you fork over money in order to take advantage of their "fantastic, once-in-a-lifetime opportunity." Here are a few ways to tell if you are working with one of these scam operations:

- First, the business asks you to hand over cash in order to work for them.

- Second, it feels to you as if the business is attempting to "sell" you something, rather than recruit you for a legitimate job.

- Third, you feel pressured and the business is attempting to push you through as soon as possible.

- Fourth, the hiring process feels disorganized, and the centralized focus is getting your fee and information as soon as humanly possible.

If it doesn't feel right, then use your gut instinct and move on.

ONE COMMON SCAM

If you have ever contacted one of these companies, it is very difficult to know who you're working with. For instance, you might have signed up under a sales arm of that company, but when you contact their customer service department, they route you to a completely different operation in an entirely different country. You will notice the obscene level of disorganization.

A very common scam that often occurs is that, once they have your email and your address, they will send out a letter with a check and certain instructions. These instructions often go along these lines:

> *Hello, we thank you for signing up with XYZ Corporation. We appreciate your willingness to help us.*
>
> *Our company is currently shipping a supply of (product) to the United States of America, and we are trying to avoid paying the full tax. We have sent you a check for $8,000. Please cash this check and deposit the amount in your bank account. Then, we ask you to wire the funds from your bank account to ours. As compensation, you may keep 10 percent for your services.*

In most cases, to someone that is looking for work, this seems like an easy way to make $800. However, what will actually happen is this:

> *You go to the check cashing company. After cashing the check, you go to your bank and deposit the funds. After depositing the funds, you approve the wire transfer and the $7,200 is sent to whatever bank they have overseas.*

Not long afterwards, you get a knock at your door from the police, because the check that you cashed twenty-four hours ago with your ID was fraudulent. Then, you find that the "company" used the information you provided on the application, along with your direct deposit and wire transfer information, to make another hefty withdrawal from your own account. The funds that were wired overseas most likely went to an offshore bank that will be very difficult to audit.

At the end of the day, you are the one that looks the most suspicious because you cashed a fraudulent check and wired the money overseas shortly thereafter. The overseas predators laugh all the way to the bank with your information and what was left in your account, and now you are under criminal investigation for check fraud and attempted tax evasion.

This sort of scam has become very commonplace in the "work-from-home" market. It is especially effective because the victim knows that he or she is "working" for a "company" that is established overseas. If the person is not aware of tax law and the possibility of check fraud, then it could land the individual in a world of financial and legal pain.

ESPECIALLY DANGEROUS

There has never been a time when Americans have faced such a threat from overseas, especially because of how small the world is in this era. Identity theft is much like a virus in that it requires a mode of transmission in order to spread. In earlier times, it was much harder to pull off (especially overseas) for the simple fact that it took quite a bit of funding and time to ensnare someone that was halfway around the world. In this case, the Internet has brought the U.S. up close and connected to the rampant criminality of many of these countries.

It is not only very easy to hide in places like India or Pakistan, but their general lack of law enforcement has enabled them to evade investigation. Even if they were investigated, the larger operations have the ability to quickly break down and set up somewhere else. This ability to dodge law enforcement makes them that much more daring and efficient in how they are able to target individuals in the U.S. and Europe.

Overall, it is important to do your homework before working with companies overseas. Even otherwise legitimate companies who are contracted with companies in the U.S. have dealt with their fair share of identity theft issues. Unfortunately, since more U.S. companies are outsourcing these days, this is becoming much harder to avoid.

It has become next to impossible to avoid identity theft, especially the kind that can strike from thousands of miles away. When there is absolutely no real warning, the results can be devastating. In the next section, we are going to discuss the best ways on how to avoid identity theft in terms of lifestyle changes.

Invisibility is the first and best way to guard yourself. If thieves cannot see their target, then they are not able to hit their target.

SECTION FOUR

The Invisibility Objective

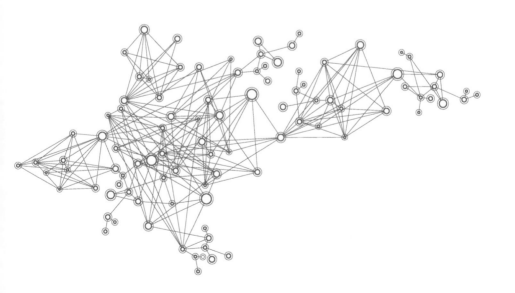

SECTION

FOUR

Chapter 15

THE INVISIBILITY OBJECTIVE: A QUICK LOOK

In this section we are going to switch gears from discussing what threats are in existence to how to keep these threats at bay.

The Invisibility Objective is not necessarily a few minor changes in life's day-to-day functions, but is rather a change in lifestyle. Because it is such a different lifestyle from the kind we are taught to live, it will likely be more difficult to accomplish for some. In any form of governance, the old understanding about liberty versus security still rings true.

In order to have liberty, one must sometimes give up security. The same is true in the opposing sense: in order to attain security, one must sacrifice liberty. Of course, in terms of lawful governance, a nation should always err on the side of liberty.

However, it is up to the individual to make the choice in living a secure life. Security, especially against identity theft, may mean making hard personal decisions that may interfere with the easy freedoms of living day to day in this modern world. It is not up to the government to decide how secure your identity should be; it is your responsibility to secure your life and the lives of those who are in your care.

STAGE ONE

The Invisibility Objective centers around a multi-stage approach at attaining the appropriate level of personal information security. The first stage is, of course, invisibility. If the prying eye cannot initially see the individual, then that individual most likely avoids becoming a target. In the same way you hide your valuables under the seat or in the trunk if your car is parked in a dark alley, the Invisibility Objective aims at hiding your identity from the possibility of attracting attention. It is this negative attention that is often the result of identity theft issues.

In addition, if you are a privacy-minded individual, then the principal of cloaking your activities from the watchful eyes of major corporate and government data mining efforts is an important one. While it is true that these major entities use highly sophisticated methods to extract your data, it is rather easy to hide your online searches, transactions, and other activities from them. Essentially, the less information they have, the better off the average citizen will be in the event of a ruling tyranny in the U.S.

This is perhaps the first and most important aspect of the Invisibility Objective for the simple fact that it is the first line of defense. The enemy cannot exploit a crack in the wall if they don't even know there is a wall (or a castle behind it).

STAGE TWO

The second part of the Invisibility Objective coincides with what we discussed in Chapter 10. In the event that an identity thief has targeted your information, then you can still repel an attempt at data extraction. By making sure that the predator does not acquire all the necessary information in order to use your identity, this will effectively stop the utilization of your name. For instance, if the thief was able to acquire your name, but not your birthplace, birthdate, or address, then your name is basically useless for their goals.

There are several methods to accomplish this, such as keeping bits and pieces of your identity isolated and in separate places. Storing everything in a single location is a surefire way to lose it all in the event that a threat breaches your initial defenses. However, keeping your personal data separated will force the predator to spend more time and energy. Not only does taking more time increase the level of risk for the predator, but the increased effort also makes the financial payoff less beneficial.

Separating the key from the lock is essential to the safety of information. While there may not be one, single way to make your identity information ironclad, putting obstacles in place will force predators through a labyrinth. This is often far better than having an impenetrable dome ...and making the mistake of thinking that it is, in fact, impenetrable. Sadly, we've learned time and time again that nothing is theft-proof. However, it is possible to make an information target far more difficult to extract than it is worth.

STAGE THREE

The third stage of the Invisibility Objective is simple: it is always important to have insurance against such a growing threat. While you might do everything in your power to hide your information and hinder thieves from extracting personal data, it is important not to underestimate how efficient predators can be (especially in an age of nonstop technological escalation).

Having a backup plan is your absolute last line of defense. This defense must be extremely strong and specific in what it protects. In addition, it is important to have multiple backups that identity thieves will not expect.

Essentially, not only do you need to protect yourself in an insurance sense, but it is crucial that you have a way of identifying the leak. Apprehending the predator will give you peace of mind in knowing that the problem is solved and not just temporarily stopped.

CONVENTIONAL PROTECTIONS

The Invisibility Objective will also highlight the physical aspect of protecting yourself. This is usually a given, as many of these tactics are being practiced by even moderately privacy-minded individuals.

The conventional protection aspect has most to do with guarding your identity through various techniques that make it more difficult for a threat to target you. Not only does this have to do with practices like shredding documents, but it also emphasizes your situational awareness in terms of who might be looking over your shoulder (and not just metaphorically speaking).

Situational awareness is the most basic principal in regards to the conventional methods of keeping your information safe. It is important to understand where your information may leak and how it might be extracted. Understanding this will naturally keep you aware to compromising situations. For instance, when you are at an ATM and there appears to be some kind of addition (new, unrecognizable equipment attached), it is best not to use it. In a more obvious sense, you would never want to leave your laptop, wallet,

credit cards, or any other sensitive information exposed and unprotected for more than a few seconds.

This aspect has more to do with forming a new understanding and awareness of the danger, and changing your lifestyle to meet the security threat.

CYBER PROTECTIONS

Keeping your information secure over the Internet and within any kind of network means that you need to equip yourself with knowledge of how identity thieves work and understand what methods they use. This is perhaps the most difficult protection to tackle. The first reason for this is due to the rather sophisticated nature of cyber protection. The second reason is because the cyber world is always changing. The best predators constantly evolve and escalate their tactics beyond the most common defenses, which means that you need to keep up with their pace (or simply avoid technology altogether).

Your cyber protections depend on how heavily you use things like social networking utilities, shop online, and even use search engines. In addition, cyber protections will cover how best to avoid identity theft on your smartphone, and also how to ensure that your home network remains secure.

Perhaps one of the most prominent aspects of cyber protections also regards corporate and government data mining efforts. Your cognizant efforts at remaining unseen while on the Internet will reduce the size of your profile and make you less of a target.

BANKING, TAXES, AND THE TYRANNY TO COME

Because the U.S. continues to slip into decline, law and order appear to continually evaporate. The freedoms and privacy that citizens once enjoyed are eroding constantly, and it is important to have an ultimate backup plan.

This, of course, might be seen as illegal in today's society. We do not support evasion of the law in any way, meaning that the tactics we will be discussing are not to be used while the U.S. remains solvent. These practices that we will mention in the coming chapters have more to do with the coming possibility of anarchy and the tyranny that will inevitably follow. In a historical sense, the inspiration for this part of the Invisibility Objective comes from past tyrannies;

however, theses tactics should not be used while the current form of the U.S. government remains in place.

Nevertheless, it is important to have a way to keep your assets safe from confiscation or theft. This will cover the possibility of using offshore banking, as well as maintaining the ability to keep mobile. In addition, we will briefly discuss how to live off grid, meaning that your electronic identity is left behind you. In this highly possible, worst-case scenario, it is important to keep from being discovered or draw attention.

This last and final aspect of the Invisibility Objective is more concerned with maintaining your quality of life in the event of a tyrannical government takeover. Whether the takeover itself is sparked by social-civil unrest, war, economic decline, or even a pandemic, it is important to keep your profile small and hard to notice. In the same way you would want to keep your profile small to repel identity thieves, you will want to implement similar practices to keep a snooping government at bay. By utilizing the Invisibility Objective to ward off both a tyrannical government and the criminal elements that will inevitably arise in the wake of that pre-tyranny state of government, you'll effectively kill two birds with one stone. Both the criminals and the government will have a hard time tracking you down at all.

However, it is very important to note that, the more you attempt to dodge attention under our current government, the more you will certainly attract attention. This is one reason why it is very important to follow our current laws to the letter. Not only is it, simply put, the right thing to do, but it is also going to keep unwanted attention away from you. If you attempt to evade detection in this era, you will only attract it. However, if you simply slip into the shadows if a major nation-changing event were to occur, then you will increase your chances of successfully disappearing. In this case, timing is everything. Using the coming changes as your diversion will not only keep you from violating today's laws, but it will cover your escape and increase your chances of success.

A CHANGE OF MIND

Again, we must emphasize that the best way to maintain a low profile is to follow the laws that are in place. It is both right and smart. In addition, we are not advocating the breakdown of law and order. In fact, it is law and order that keeps our property (our identities) safe. The absolute worst case scenario is anarchy; while the second-worst is tyranny.

Also, unlike many in the patriot community, we do not feel as if it is a smart idea to draw attention to ourselves (especially if we are trying to maintain a small profile). Unfortunately, this is not Boston in 1775. The British didn't have drones, the NSA, or a world police force. The world has changed. There are times when the best of us must evaporate, let the disaster run its course, and then resurface when the time is right. This, of course, is for those of us who intend to hide in order to keep ourselves and our loved ones in safety.

However, we are not saying that it is wrong for someone to stand up, use his or her First Amendment liberties, and shout from the rooftops. It is correct that our government is clearly treading a dangerous path and society is following like sheep to the slaughterhouse. There are wrongs that must be blasted through the bullhorn. However, it is important that whoever courageously takes up the bullhorn must understand the danger. You will not be able to hide and you will become a target. Of course, while we urge you to adopt the principles discussed in the Invisibility Objective, they may only get you so far. When the watchful eyes of malevolent entities are upon you, it is difficult to hide. This is precisely why the Invisibility Objective is best utilized for folks who aren't necessarily interested in changing today, but want to invest in tomorrow.

FIRST THINGS FIRST

Much of this book is written to prepare your mind for implementing the Invisibility Objective in your life. Understanding the most basic principles and liberties of privacy, the private entity threats that exist, and the tyranny that is already installing its control grid is one of the most crucial aspects of changing our lifestyles to meet the personal information security threat.

The gravity of our present situation is tectonically shifting for the worst, and the rate of the shift is picking up speed. Our time to prepare is short, and this is why we must renew our minds quickly so we can be ready when the world does its worst against us. Had the Jewish (and minority) population in Europe taken the appropriate protective action before the Nazi regime implemented its campaign of death against the innocent, millions may have saved themselves rather than depending on their salvation from allied forces when it was too late.

Bearing these threats in mind will produce a healthy, productive fear. It is this productivity that will move you towards protecting yourselves, rather than dangerously ignoring the threats to come. The Invisibility Objective is a response to reality, not fantasy. Its implementation is an active, protective response for our survival.

Chapter 16

INVISIBILITY OBJECTIVE: CONVENTIONAL METHODS

In this chapter, we discuss the basics on how to protect your identity from predators (private, corporate, and government). Those who are reading this book are most likely already using many of the methods discussed in this section, and many of the methods have already been mentioned in previous chapters. However, it is always important to review the basics. Essentially, we will mostly be discussing the conventional methods of stages one, two, and three of the Invisibility Objective. All three stages will be mentioned in each chapter of this section, but each subsequent chapter will cover the different areas of implementation (conventional, cyber, and the tyranny to come).

STAGE ONE

The first phase of being able to secure your information through conventional means comes from your situational awareness and your understanding of how the danger imposes itself in your life. How to become invisible has to do with how you interact with the possibility of these dangers.

The first step you will need to take is to figure out where your personal information leaks will take place. For instance, you will need to go through your papers, safes, dresser drawers, etc., and locate all of your paperwork. One of the fastest ways to risk identity theft is by not knowing where your papers and plastic are located. This is one of the most fundamental parts of Stage One, for the simple fact that it is, perhaps, the most easily overlooked, but the first exploited by identity theft predators.

Make a list of the paperwork that you need to find. In addition, if you are a parent or caring for someone, it is important that you locate your loved one's paperwork as well. The list provided below is not necessarily exhaustive, but these tend to be the most used by identity thieves:

- Social Security card

- Birth certificate

- Bills

- Bank account information (checks, statements, slips, etc.)

- Passports

- Employment applications

- Government identification (driver's licenses, visas, etc.)

- Credit cards and statements

- Car registration

- Insurance information, cards, and policies (car, renters, homeowners, life, etc.)

- Tax information

- Anything else that has information that can be used by identity thieves in methods previously discussed.

Locating this kind of paperwork is absolutely essential for the simple fact that, if any of it is lost, then that opens the door to the possibility of it being found (but not by you). This is basically your act of tying off your loose ends, securing and identifying the source of information, and then protecting it.

Once you have all the information gathered together, then it is time to plan on where to stash it with the Invisibility Objective in mind.

CHANGES IN INTERACTION

In the same way you are gathering up your info and preventing others from seeing it, you will also need to ensure that your information is not seen when you are interacting with society. Here are several awareness tips that you should bear in mind when in public or even in your home:

- Trust in very few people. Sadly, a massive amount of identity theft is perpetrated by the folks who are closely related or acquainted with the victim. Roommates, spouses, children, parents, friends, and coworkers are not exempt from this list. It is up to you to make the decision on who is trustworthy and more importantly, who is not.

In addition, even if you do trust the individual with your identity information, it may not be a smart idea to entrust this information if he or she is unaware of the risks. For instance, your son or daughter may unwittingly hand over your credit card information to a predator over the phone. While it wasn't necessarily the child's identity theft, the predator was still able to extract the information from him or her.

- When you are in a restaurant, coffee shop, or at a store, be sure to be aware of who is behind you, especially when producing any of the documentation listed above. Because of tactics like shoulder surfing, identity thieves can extract your information by simply looking over your shoulder (hence the name). So, if you are in public, be aware of who is behind you, near you, and even notice who may be acting strangely and curiously observant in close proximity.

- Never leave your information unattended. For instance, if you are at a coffee shop and you need to leave the room and your laptop, then either ask someone to watch your things, or simply pack it up and take it with you. However, be aware that the person you ask to watch your things may also not be trustworthy. Sometimes it is simply best not to part with any of your items that contain personal data.

- Avoid giving your personal information over the phone and especially through email. If you are in a position where you cannot help it, then be sure to ask for the other person's work information so that you might track down the leak if something were to happen. For instance, if you are working with a company, then write down the full name of the person on the other end of the line. If identity theft does occur, you will have the name of the person who may have accidentally given a predator your information. Also, the customer service person may be a predator as well, so make sure you have a way of tracking down where the leak took place. Though sometimes, this situation is unavoidable.

- If anyone comes into physical contact with your credit cards or social security number, keep their names in mind and the time of the transaction. For instance, we mentioned the pizza delivery driver scenario: be sure to remember the time of the transaction and the driver's name in order to track down the leak in the event of an identity theft. Again, if the employee makes you uncomfortable (possibly by the long duration and curious handling of your information), then be sure to let the place of business know what happened. It is better to be secure than to be attacked, no matter how trivial the situation may seem.

- Keep your information out of sight, and produce it only when you must. Again, you will most likely have to produce this information on a daily basis, but once you are finished with it, put it back into your purse or pocket. The longer your information is out, the higher the chances of unsavory characters extracting the information.

- In addition, it is important that you completely destroy any personal information you no longer need. You should either shred or burn old letters, bank statements, credit card statements, medical bills, tax documents (which you no longer need), etc. Also be sure to cut up old

credit cards, debit cards, insurance cards, and don't throw them all away in a single trashcan. For this kind of information, you will need to move to Stage Two and begin to build your labyrinth.

STAGE TWO

It is important to construct your labyrinth in such a way that you disable others from finding your information, while enabling yourself to quickly access it. Also, as we mentioned in the last chapter, you need to be sure to separate the key from the lock. The advantage is the fact that, in the event of an information breech, the identity thief must jump through several hoops in order to obtain the personal data that he or she was looking for.

You can do this in several ways. This method will depend on your life situation, so there is no one foolproof method by which this will work:

- As we mentioned above, when disposing of personal information, do so in a way that a potential identity thief cannot simply take a single plastic bag from your trashcan. You may want to dispose of the information over a long period of time (multiple weeks), or find other trashcans and dispose of it all at once.

- Never keep all of your important documents, plastic cards, tax information, government identification, etc., in the same place. This is only asking for trouble. You should keep each major form of documentation in its own safe place. However, you can keep topics of information together. For instance, you can keep all of your bank statements in one place, as simply finding all of them together will only reveal a certain part of the information, while not revealing anything else. It is much like finding several identical puzzle pieces, but none of which will recreate the rest of the puzzle.

At the same time, you should never keep your Social Security card in the same place as your birth certificate, as a thief can quickly use this information to his or her advantage, thereby completing the puzzle. Be sure to have separate safe caches of your information, and do not write down where it is located, as it is best to keep this information memorized. It is also best to keep lock boxes and safes for storing your personal documents and data, and keep them in hard-to-reach and hard-to-find places. Thus, if an identity thief comes prowling, it will be next to impossible and take far too long to acquire his or her targets.

- Have multiple places on your person where you can keep information. However, try to separate your identification from your credit cards. So, keep your ID in a bag, while your credit cards remain in your wallet or purse. This will ensure that if your wallet gets stolen, the thief won't have your identification. Also, if your bag gets stolen, they won't have your credit cards.

- Do not keep any information in the glove box of your vehicle. Glove boxes are great for tire pressure gauges and ...well, gloves. Almost every driver in the U.S. will keep his or her car registration and insurance information in the glove box. If your car is broken in to, you have leaked mountains of information very quickly for the simple fact that your information was kept in the most obvious place.

Instead, keep your registration information and car insurance information under two separate seats. Not only will this separate two sets of important documents, but acquiring them will look awkward and finding them will take time. The more time and the more effort it takes for a thief, the higher the risk and likelihood of getting caught in the act. There is even a good chance that if a would-be identity thief were to break into the vehicle and find no information in the glove box, then he or she is likely to stop looking and assume you don't have any in the car.

- Last, if you feel your information has been compromised, even on the slightest suspicion, then simply move your pieces to different and random locations. You may also want to get into the practice of doing this once every two months, just to ensure your information's security. Do not move your information in predictable cycles, as unpredictability can add even more challenge to the labyrinth you are constructing.

Note: For some ideas on building hides for your valuables, check out Solutions From Science's book, How to Hide Your Guns. There are tons of suggestions for constructing places or utilizing what's available to keep your valuable papers out of the hands of criminals. Go to www.hideyourguns.com.

Another helpful tip for protecting your information is to keep a mugger's wallet. Travel savvy individuals who make frequent trips overseas will use this method, especially in high-crime areas. A mugger's wallet is full of cheap, fake novelty IDs and credit cards, only a few dollars, and the wallet itself is very inexpensive. When being mugged, instead of handing them the real thing, the victim throws the mugger's wallet past the criminal. Because the mugger has little interest in the victim and only wants the wallet, he will most likely turn to get it, giving the victim a chance to sprint away from the situation and call the police. By the time the mugger realizes that the IDs and credit cards are fake, the victim is long gone.

Bear in mind, decoys are a very wonderful and powerful deterrent. If the identity thief unwittingly happens upon a decoy, then they are most likely going to leave. Again, once the thief realizes that the decoy is not the real thing, it is far too late.

STAGE THREE

Having insurance against these types of problems is always a smart idea. There are many companies out there who specialize in the prevention of identity theft and rebuilding their customer's lives if a theft were to take place.

Again, it is impossible to keep out all identity theft, meaning that it is a smart idea to invest in companies that can help you keep this issue at bay. One of the best things that identity theft prevention companies do is that they insure the customer. For instance, if an identity thief does $500,000 in damages to the victim, then the identity theft company will compensate their customer for that amount.

However, all of these companies have the means by which to monitor bank accounts, credit scores, and other databases for suspicious activity. Once something is tripped, the company then puts their system into overdrive. Not only do they make an effort to quickly stop the identity theft from going any further, but oftentimes, their work leads to the apprehension of the perpetrator. Apprehending the perpetrator largely means that the leak is plugged, and the victim can move on.

Also, for Stage Three, is important to note that you may need to change your Social Security number and other information in the event that a theft took place. Thus, if you lost your wallet, you may want to go to your local DMV and get a new driver's license (with different information), go to the Social Security office and get a new number, etc. Be sure to cancel your credit cards and change all other information that was kept in the wallet. It is crucial that you stop any leaks, even before they take place. Yes, your wallet may never be found, but you may not want to take the chance of it being found by someone with malicious intent.

However, this is another function of identity theft prevention companies: some actually have lost or stolen wallet protection. For instance, all you need to do is let them know of the theft, and they will go to work monitoring for fraudulent charges and cancel any fraudulent transactions that may take place. In addition, they will cover traveler's checks, personal checks, driver's licenses, etc.

You may want to shop around for the best identity theft prevention companies, but we do highly recommend using their services once you've found one that is right for you.

SUMMARY

These are some of the more basic methods of protecting yourself from identity theft, and we do understand that many people are already putting these methods into practice. However, it is important that you implement the majority of these tips into your life.

Essentially, having backups to your backups will not only deter identity theft, but it will make you far more difficult of a target than you are likely worth to the identity thief. Implementing the methods that make your information invisible and constructing a labyrinth within your life is a double-barrier of protection that most identity thieves have never come across.

However, even if a predator is quite resourceful and he or she is able to make it through your elaborate system of protection, then having backup alerts and insurance through an identity theft prevention company will be a virtually unbreakable third protection. Statistically speaking, if you implement all three stages of the Invisibility Objective in your life, then there is a solid chance that your bouts with identity theft will be short, easy, and very rare. Even if the identity thief was able to make off with loads of money, you're insured and will be compensated.

However, these are some of the most basic methods by which everyone should protect his or her identity from the common identity thief, and the predators are constantly evolving. In the old days, predators use to extract this information from our papers and effects, but now they are extracting the information through cyber space. Higher advancement in identity theft requires higher advancement in identity theft prevention techniques. And so, we move on to the advanced methods for keeping out of sight and remaining secure in the digital world.

Chapter 17

INVISIBILITY OBJECTIVE: ADVANCED METHODS

In this chapter of the Invisibility Objective, we will discuss the advanced methods in terms of how to protect your personal information in cyber space. This is going to be, perhaps, the most difficult aspect of the Invisibility Objective, because it is the easiest to overlook. At the same time, because society continues to move faster and faster to the conveniences of doing business online, the most proficient identity thieves have evolved to meet these new opportunities.

It is important to understand that cyber space is always changing, which means the cons are evolving with it. This also means that we have a responsibility to evolve with them in order to prepare for the information security threat they impose. Underestimating even the novices in the criminal community usually results in becoming a victim, so it is important to take the steps to protect yourself against the best of them.

Our approach in this chapter is two-fold. First, we will help guide you on how to protect yourself against the common tech-savvy identity thief. Second, we will show you how to evade the watchful eyes of data mining companies. Because we know that it is largely through data mining companies that the U.S. government is able to track American citizens, simply keeping out the data miners is a surefire way to lessen the size of your profile, and make you harder to notice. Overall, the key is to be prepared for any eventuality coming your way from any direction—and unfortunately, in the cyber world, there are enemies coming at you from many directions simultaneously.

The old saying still rings true in this age of cyber identity theft crime: "Hope for the best; prepare for the worst."

STAGE ONE

Your first goal in protecting yourself online is to become invisible to folks who may be in search of your information. Covering your tracks is key for the simple fact that the predators cannot hunt who they cannot see. In the same way you would want to cover your tracks when attempting to evade an aggressor in the wilderness, you want to do the same with your computer and smartphone usage.

One of the biggest ways to cover your tracks online is to understand how Internet cookies work. Cookies can be loosely defined as text identifiers that are loaded onto your browser that allow websites to track your specific machine on their server. When you return, they know it is you.

Online search companies such as Google and Yahoo use cookies and other sophisticated methods for tracking your online usage, which make them highly proficient at mining your data. This is how they can tell not only what you're doing, but who you are as a person (as we discussed previously). When one company can track your searches to a point where they know what types of websites you go to, what you buy online, and how long you spend time there, they can then extract this information and analyze it using mathematical and psychological algorithms. Essentially, this gives them unique knowledge on what you are going to do or think before it even crosses your mind.

Identity thieves work on a much smaller level, slipping into your system when your guard is down, and extract necessary bits and pieces of information. In many cases, this needs to be done on a more local level, and their net is much smaller. If you are a target, then more pressure will be applied to finding your machine. Then it is only a matter of time before they are able to force it open or trick you into letting them in (the latter of which is more likely going to happen).

As we mentioned before, most identity thieves need to be able to find your system. Essentially, this is done in two ways. The first way is to cast a net in hopes of finding someone who unwittingly wanders by. The second way is to target a single priority individual. Either way, the key is in not making yourself a target by staying low and utilizing protections that are already in place, but regularly neglected.

For instance, in most cases, various establishments have already put protections in place to keep identity thieves at bay. They simply don't want their customers to be scared away because of problems with identity theft. Not only is it bad for business, it may also legally involve their company in the process. So, many online companies use SSL in order to keep outside parties from infiltrating and stealing sensitive information during a transaction.

SSL (or Secure Socket Layer) is basically a conduit by which you can contact the company's website without fear of someone monitoring what you are doing. An SSL encrypts your information, meaning that whoever may be attempting to watch what is going on is not going to be able to read things like your credit card number. You can see that you are using an SSL website by looking at the URL bar. If the URL says "https://", then you are in SSL. In addition, you will often find a padlock icon somewhere on your browser screen.

If you are shopping online, you can be fairly certain that you won't have problems with hackers taking a peek at your transactions when you are using SSL. Of course, not all encryptions are created equally, and some hackers can crack them (but the ones that have this capability are usually working for the Pentagon or for IT companies).

Essentially, the only real tip for you is to avoid doing online transactions with companies who don't use SSL. If you don't see the "s" in "https://" don't make the transaction, and back away quickly. There's a big chance that you weren't the only one to notice and unfortunately, when predators smell blood in the air, they go on the prowl.

SSL essentially makes you invisible to an identity thief, which means that doing online transactions through SSL security is not just a nice security perk, it's essential.

In the same way that identity thieves throw out a net and hope someone unwittingly swims by through monitoring unprotected online storefronts, they will also attempt to locate their prey by enticing them into traps. Phishing is a practice whereby an identity thief will blast out emails, chats, messages, or whatever to trick people into entering their information.

For example, a highly proficient phisher will blast out an email campaign to 100,000 people, making them believe that Verizon is doing a survey. On this survey, the customer has to enter information such as a social security number, address, phone number, date of birth, etc. While the vast majority wouldn't enter this information had it been an actual Verizon survey (and most would recognize it to be a phishing campaign), there are those 100 people who will fill out the information thoroughly.

In another style of phishing scheme, the identity thief will spend time researching his or her target. This scheme is called spear phishing, as they will attempt to learn about the target, and then bait the individual with highly relevant and personalized contact (personal emails from "known contacts" and such). This is a very difficult kind of attack to stop, but it is only focused on one victim.

One of the best ways to ensure that you are not attacked by a phishing scheme is to make sure that your tracks are covered while using the Internet. Phishing schemes are operated based on how many contacts they can extract from various databases. For instance, your information is often extracted by data mining companies through cookies.

Identity thieves will then buy this information (emails, addresses, names, etc.), and exploit it with phishing schemes. Unfortunately, some of these lists of contact information are stolen or extracted through illegal means, making avoidance of this scheme somewhat difficult. Ultimately, the key is simply not to blindly trust in the validity of the emails you receive. If you are ever contacted by a company and asked to provide information, either contact that company by phone and ask if the email or message is valid, or simply do not respond.

The same goes for smartphone applications. It is absolutely crucial that you do not open or install any applications that you did not prompt or find on your own. If you receive an email from an unknown contact (or even a known one for that matter), and that email asks you to install an application (even if you recognize it), simply do not trust it. As we mentioned before, this is a quick way to allow an identity thief into your phone to extract your information or hijack it altogether. You do not always know who sent the message or for what purpose, even if you recognize the sender. The most effective hackers can wear many masks. Only install applications from known, official sources, and only if you know for sure that a known associate sent the email. Always think twice about these kinds of contact.

Also, surfing the Internet through using anonymous means will lessen your risk of your contact information landing in a list that is exploited by phishers. As we mentioned before, data mining companies can build databases of contact information by leaving cookies on your browser. Then, they sell this information to companies for marketing purposes. Unfortunately, not all those companies are real ones.

A fantastic tool to making yourself invisible while surfing the Web is by using search engines like StartPage.com, which is powered by Ixquick. Ixquick is one of the few search engines that does not record your information in any way, as this is one of the hallmarks of their company. In addition, through StartPage.com, Ixquick can actually allow you to utilize Google searches (but remain anonymous), by sending your search through a proxy server. Basically, it's directing a third party to do a search, and that third party will not give out your name when asked. Also, Ixquick is compatible with SSL web applications, meaning that you will not lose any online surfing or shopping capabilities, but you will be a ghost while using it.

Essentially, using sites like StartPage.com will enable you to anonymously browse the Internet, meaning that you will no longer end up in data mining company lists. They will not know your name or your IP address, and they can't save cookies to your hard drive.

Being invisible in cyberspace is rather easy, if you simply know the basics on how to cover your tracks. Using companies like Ixquick is a fantastic way to accomplish 40 percent of maintaining online anonymity. Common sense comprises 60 percent. In most cases, if you are only using SSL for online transactions and only using anonymous browsing search engines, you will likely cut your chances of being attacked to astronomically small odds.

STAGE TWO (A): NETWORKS AND PASSWORDS

For the second stage of protecting yourself against cyber identity theft, it is important to put additional protections in place. Unfortunately, building a labyrinth is going to be difficult, especially since the average privacy-minded individual does not have near the level of technological skill that most hackers do.

However, the key here is to make sure that your protections make you more difficult a target than the average person. Once the predators see that you are more difficult to attack, they will likely move on to easier prey who don't take as much time and energy.

First and foremost, much of your surfing and online transactions will take place at home. This means that you should strengthen your home network, especially if you are running wireless Internet. Anyone can purchase a Wi-Fi repeater, a device that can take in a wireless signal and expand the area of broadcast. This means that a predator doesn't need to be sitting outside your house or next door to cut into your network. Depending on the repeater, they can be down the street.

We aren't going to go into a high level of detail, as different operating systems will have different ways of doing things. We are simply going to go into the basics. Naturally, you will want to place as many headaches between the hacker and your network as possible. After spending too much time, they may simple give up and try a different network if you aren't their priority target.

First, it is important that you assign a password to your wireless router. This can often be done when setting up your router, or by finding your gateway IP address. If you are confused on how to do this, give the manufacturer of your router a call, and they should walk you through the steps.

Once you do this, you will want to encrypt your network. Your network will likely default to a WEP encryption; however, this type has been proven to be rather easily cracked. Unfortunately, there are cheap programs that anyone can download that will be able to crack a WEP encryption within minutes. You will want to use a WPA or WPA2 level encryption, which will be much harder for a hacker to break. Be sure that you write down the information from your key once you get the encryption up and running.

After that, you will want to turn on your firewall. Many operating systems already come with firewalls, meaning that in most cases, all you need to do is turn it on. Then find out the MAC addresses of the devices you want to approve for your network. Interestingly enough, you should be able to find out what other devices are using your network through seeing how many MAC addresses have logged on. If you see an extra one, you might want to investigate, because someone unauthorized may currently be on your network. A firewall is simply an added protection that only accepts devices into the network with the MAC addresses that you previously approved.

Again, we do realize that for the average person, this probably sounds like jargon-mumbo-jumbo-hacker talk. However, the instructions by which to accomplish this are all over the Internet, and you can certainly call the manufacturer of your router who will walk you through the steps of making your home network ironclad.

However, the most important part about making your devices secure is being sure to have a solid set of passwords. If you are using a simple password or the same password for multiple devices and accounts, then you place yourself at incredible risk.

Here are a few criteria for passwords that will stump the best of them:

- Do not use any part of your name or the names of anyone who are in your care.

- Do not use birth dates (as identity thieves are likely going to know this information already).

- Do not use addresses.

- Do not use important dates (anniversaries, graduations, etc.)

- Do not use a word or phrase that describes something about you that the general public may know about.

- It is best to use a random word or name.

- Use a series of upper and lowercase characters.

- Use numbers and other characters if the system authorizes you to do so.

- Change your passwords at least once every two months.

- Again, do NOT use the same password for multiple devices or accounts.

Following these rules will keep a hacker at bay for quite a while, especially since so many people use badly devised sets of passwords. It is crucial that your passwords do not fall into the wrong hands, meaning that you should trust only the people who value your information's security as much as you do. Entrusting your password to someone who doesn't, while they may have no malicious intent, may accidentally give it up to someone who does have malicious intent.

Your passwords are often the last line of defense against highly efficient identity thieves and hackers for the simple fact that they can crack an encryption. It's often difficult to crack a well-thought out password, however.

Bear in mind, though, that passwords can be cracked through various methods. There are ways to bypass a password system, and there are even ways to break through, but those methods are usually carried out by highly accomplished hackers who are really spending a good deal of time and energy on a specific target. Unfortunately, no system is unbreakable with enough time, energy, and know-how.

For hackers who aren't as proficient, they can still often get into your devices. This is usually accomplished by you unknowingly letting them in. In many cases, a hacker will load a program on to your system through baiting you into opening an email that they sent you. Once the email is opened, the program (virus) installs on to your computer. In many cases, they can completely hijack the device itself, and the only control you will have is the off switch, unplugging it, or removing the battery.

In a more direct approach, there are devices called keystroke recorders. Keystroke recorders must be plugged into a USB port manually; however, some recorders will actually wirelessly broadcast your keystrokes. This means that a hacker can easily extract a password. The only drawback with this method for the hacker is the fact that he or she must actually break in or trick you into installing the device.

This is why it is absolutely crucial for you to know your equipment and know how to locate any suspicious hardware. It is important to learn about network security, as your information's security depends on it.

STAGE TWO (B): COMMON SENSE PRACTICES

In this second part of stage two, we want to cover the common sense practices concerning securing the devices that hold so much of our personal information. Basically, these are things that everyone should understand and will simply make it that much harder for an identity thief to track down your information once you've been identified.

Of course, you may be fine with walking away from a book, cup of coffee, a jacket, or even a note pad when you're at a coffee shop. You should never walk away from your phone or your laptop. Keeping these devices in your sight is the first step to making sure that they don't get stolen, because unfortunately, a stolen device will inevitably divulge all of its information in a rather short amount of time. A lost smartphone is far worse than a lost credit card, because your smartphone likely has information about multiple credit cards, multiple bank accounts, your address, your date of birth, your account information with your data provider, your emails, and just about anything else that can put you in a world of hurt if it ended up in the wrong hands.

Simply put, keep your devices to yourself, and only allow those you trust to have access to them.

Also, be sure to keep track of how much information you post online. Identity thieves, hackers, con artists, common thieves, and the like all have one thing in common: they think outside rules and laws. This means that they are often highly intelligent and highly motivated. So, do be careful when posting pictures, statuses, locations, etc., online for the simple fact that someone may be watching.

For instance, you might have just posted that you are on vacation. What better time for an identity thief to break into your home, install a wireless keystroke recorder, and then wait for you to get home and log into your network?

The most basic principle when dealing with cyberspace is to trust no one. If you are working with a company online, be sure to do research on their business. If you are asked to provide information, verify that they are who they say they are before cooperating. Simply put, when online, a person can become anyone with enough time, knowledge, and resources. You do not always know whom you are talking to, and you do not always know who may be watching you.

STAGE THREE

To date, there aren't many real options for insurance against cyber threats. While you may be able to hire an IT professional to build up your network's security, there aren't really any companies that will insure against an attack. At this point, the first winds of hacker insurance coverage is still more of a rumor on a news page than anything else. And even if these insurance companies are just beginning to make their debut, you would need to have a $10 million network infrastructure to protect in order to make coverage worth it.

Stage three in advanced methods is more concerned about stopping the leaks, especially since the Invisibility Objective's basic methods in stage three included the necessary insurance to compensate the actual financial damage done.

For example, say a hacker breaks into your system and steals your credit card information, date of birth, address, etc., and then proceeds to drain your accounts dry and sets up three mortgages in your name. Having identity theft protection insurance would compensate you for that kind of damage. Actual hacker insurance would have more to do with compensating you for the damage to your network infrastructure and for most average folks, that's not going to be much.

However, one of the main reasons why we suggested setting up a firewall and getting to know your router is because you can often track down any extra device on your network. This will not only assist the police in tracking down the identity theft suspect from the IT angle, but from the other angle, your identity theft protection company would track down the suspect from the transactions he or she has been making in your name. The most important part about this is stopping the leak so the information stops leaking.

One of the most interesting ways that you can secure your devices is by installing theft-tracking software on your smartphone or laptop. Basically, if your laptop is stolen, once the thief logs on to the Internet through your device, you can actually pinpoint their exact location and lead the authorities right to them. Also, these programs will keep your Wi-Fi on and grabbing for the nearest available source. In addition, some programs will allow you to shut down access to your important information, meaning that even if the thief steals the device, he or she still can't access the good stuff.

The fun part is the fact that you can literally see in real time what the thief is doing on your computer, so if he or she logs into their Facebook, checks their email, etc., then you can find out exactly who they are. In addition, you can also turn on your own webcam and see the thief on your computer. Simply take a snapshot and hand it over to the authorities. In fact, you would know more about them than they know about you at this point. This service is available for smartphones, computers, and even tablets.

It is also very important that you back up your hard drive in the event of a successful breach or theft of your device. There are many companies out there that can do an automated backup through the Internet, but bear in mind that if the hacker were able to get hold of your password information, that backed-up data may be compromised as well. If you do have suspicions that your system has been breached, call the company immediately and ask them to reset the security information.

However, the only real way to get to your backed up information is through the hacker cracking your password into your account and even then, if the information back up company is noticing the access from an unknown IP address, the hacker will likely have to know your security questions. That may throw them a curveball that they can't hit. Thus, other than a password crack, you should not have to worry about your information being compromised from their system. Companies like CrashPlan and Carbonite have some of the most unbreakable systems devised, and their security measures rival the IT protections of modern militaries.

In addition, you may just want to keep your most crucial information backed up on an external hard drive. This hard drive must be protected, especially since you are trying to back up important personal information. It would be smart to keep this in a lockbox or safe, much the way you would store your important documents.

In this chapter we largely discussed how to stop private identity thieves from accessing your valuable personal information, how to slip them up if they are able to locate you, and last, how to catch them if they are successful. However, while we briefly discussed data mining companies in this chapter, we are going to go into even more detail on how to maintain invisibility from their watchful eyes in the next chapter. The biggest reason why it is important to reduce your profile in the records of data mining operations is because this is exactly what the power-elite military industrial complex is using.

The less they know about you, your beliefs, your friends, your family, and who you are, the less likely you will become a target. In the next two chapters, we will go into the final phases of the Invisibility Objective by evading the larger, more dangerous predators: corporations and the governments who serve them.

Chapter 18

PRESERVING YOUR PRIVACY LIBERTIES

The next two chapters will be, perhaps, the two most controversial in this book, as they have to do with how your privacy interacts with the local, state, and federal government. While many believe that privacy is merely subject to the whims of the magistrate, we understand that this view is erroneous. As we mentioned in the beginning chapters of this book, your privacy is your liberty, your right, and it is in your keeping.

Of course, some will say that if you have nothing to hide, then you should not be worried about the government, through data mining corporations, snooping upon your life. However, at the same time, the government often cries, "This is for your protection," and, "It's a matter of national security," any time they have a shameful secret that seems quite relevant to national dialogue. If they are allowed to cover up their secrets, while taking peeks at ours, then that power can run amok in a very short amount of time. The Fourth Amendment of the Constitution is clear that the government should only know about you what it is legally allowed to see. The evolution of policy should never trump law, meaning that the government is actively attempting to circumvent the Constitution, disregard common liberties, and hold your privacy hostage through the public's fear of terrorism.

At the same time, we have also explored the fact that the fourth branch of government, the military-industrial complex bureaucracy, has already sent their spies, their cameras, and all the tracking capabilities technologically available to them, and we know that the spies go before the army. Their feeling of the necessity to spy upon the population indicates their sentiments about the American population—we are the enemy. In the same way that Edward Snowden was considered an enemy of the state when he divulged the out-of-control government snooping programs perpetrated by the NSA that have been unleashed upon the common American, we ourselves are considered a threat to their power. Snowden was not giving secrets to other foreign powers. His purpose was to give this knowledge to the American people, so that we could decide what to do next. The fact that the U.S. labeled Snowden a traitor, and the fact that, by definition, a traitor is someone who assists an enemy, means that the U.S. government thinks of the American people as the enemy.

Knowing this, it is important to act in self-preservation. Deciding to live a life of privacy is not an act of war, but it is an act of lawful neutrality. We do not advocate evasion of the law. However, we do believe that it is necessary for the liberty of individuals to learn how to evade a law-breaking government.

LET'S GET THE OBVIOUS OUT OF THE WAY

Unfortunately, if the strength of the military-industrial complex was up against an individual, then that individual will most likely be found. The reason why operatives are able to go off grid is not only because they've had the training to do so, but because they also have the funding and resources.

This is not quite the case with the common privacy-minded individual American. Unfortunately, the resources of the power-elite are quite vast at this point, and if they wanted to find someone, they would have no problem doing so. Between data mining operations, reading texts, emails, and social networking utility communications, as well as drones, satellites, infrared technology, and the ability to track an RFID chip in your credit card, there really is nowhere to go if you are considered a target.

Essentially, you would have to leave anything electronically connected to you behind you, and walk, not drive, to a place where you will not be seen by cameras, make any transactions, or pay any taxes. You would have to hunt and grow all of your own food. Indeed, this may one day end up being something you are forced to do in the event that you are a refugee. However, while we are still attempting to live functioning lives in society, we have to take an accurate, real-life look at what we can and cannot do. No, slipping totally off grid would be nearly impossible for the average individual. However, it is still possible to avoid drawing attention to yourself and your family.

Ultimately, this section of the Invisibility Objective is more concerned with the idea of avoidance of becoming a target, rather than attempting to be a target that disappears. In fact, a disappearing person would draw more attention than a neutral, uninteresting individual. It is far safer to be the latter.

However, sometimes the latter is no longer an option. That is what will be discussed in the next chapter.

In this chapter, we are primarily concerned with stages one and two, as we will be discussing how to achieve a certain level of invisibility, as well as making it more difficult for you to be tracked if your demographic comes under a certain level of scrutiny. We are going to cover the extensive nature of stage three in the next chapter, as this will guide you to your ultimate backup plan against an over-zealous, tyrannical government. In this chapter, we will teach you how to be difficult to find. In the next, we will teach you the basics on how to evaporate during an all-out takeover of liberty and obliteration of the rule of law.

STAGE ONE—THE DEVIL DOESN'T KNOW YOU'RE THERE

One rather interesting anomaly about how the U.S. was founded was the fact that it originally began as a federalized system of government, born out of thirteen separate and rather independently governed colonies. The very nature of this federal government was that the states and the central government shared equal power when the Constitution was ratified in 1787. This was upset after the Civil War to a certain extent, but the power to track the entire U.S. population has largely been a logistical nightmare for the federal government.

Simply put, the separations of power, the checks and balances, and the fortunate level of disorganization has made the effort to keep tabs on single individuals a very difficult proposition. This is one reason why so many individuals can get lost in the system and fall through the cracks. The fact that the U.S. government can't seem to keep track of voters, populations, taxes, etc., says volumes about how inefficient they really are.

However, it is not the U.S. government that is the problem. It is the U.S.-based military-industrial complex that is the problem. Most of these departments and agencies are run out of the Executive branch of government, but they seem to have taken on a life of their own.

They began to realize that the U.S. government was inefficient and that the public sector had too few resources and innovations to accomplish its goal of keeping track of the population. This is why they looked to private corporations for the ability to do what they could not.

The anomaly is the fact that, where the U.S. government seems to stand alone, there is a rather high level of anonymity for the individual. It is when the U.S. government and its bureaucracy utilizes highly efficient private corporations that we find ourselves being effectively tracked. This is why, when Snowden leaked how the NSA is using companies like Verizon, Google, and Facebook, did these things finally make sense. Snowden was the Rosetta stone to understanding what the government actually knows about individuals in the U.S. population.

This is also another reason why we emphasize the dangers of data mining corporations and social networking utilities, not only from an identity theft perspective, but also from their overarching effort to invade the privacy of law-abiding citizens.

Stage one is concerned with the invisibility of the individual and is largely discussed in terms of how to avoid being tracked by data mining corporations, rather than the U.S. government as a whole. If you can maintain the ability to remain invisible to private entities, then there is a chance that you have reduced the size of your profile to the U.S. government itself, while still living a totally law-abiding life.

As we learned in the summer of 2013, perhaps the most tracked aspect of the American population is Internet usage, texts, emails, GPS, pictures, and social networking utilities, especially Facebook. The government has been doing this by extracting this information through data mining companies and other corporations through agreements with the NSA and other agencies.

Thus, the biggest factor to limiting the size of your profile is to either not use them (which should always be considered as an option), or by utilizing providers that operate through proxy servers.

In the last chapter, we mentioned a company called Ixquick and their website called StartPage. Again, not only will using this service make your online activity untraceable for hackers, but it will also make you very difficult to trace for the military-industrial complex. If you are not openly using search engines like Google or Yahoo through your own IP address, then they can't report your activity to the federal government, meaning that the government will be able to learn very little about you.

The second way that government usually pegs someone they want to start watching is by tracking purchases. This is one of the first parts of a suspect's life that is monitored during a criminal investigation, so naturally, it is one of the first parts of your life that you need to make a privacy priority. Simply put, learn to operate on cash. This isn't always easy, especially if you do a lot of shopping online, but learning to work with cash is the fastest way to keep your purchases to yourself. In addition, it will keep companies like Visa, MasterCard, Discover, etc., as well as your bank from knowing who you are as a person, and they will only know your basic information (information the government should already know). The more you can work with cash, the less data you give them to work with.

We do understand that this isn't always possible, especially when paying the usual bills. But keep in mind that just about everyone pays bills such as rent, mortgage, taxes, insurance, and utilities, so this will not make you stick out. However, if you purchase ammunition with your debit card, you can be fairly certain that federal agencies will learn about it.

In addition, we will further discuss the advantages of cash in the next chapter when we cover the third stage of privacy in relation to the government.

STAGE TWO—COMMUNICATION LABYRINTH

Since the government has been exposed for tracking emails, it is crucially important for us to cover them up as well. Fortunately, there are ways to send and receive emails anonymously. However, this method requires discipline. It is rather complicated and will not work with usual business, since the text of the emails may include your information. Rather, this method is best suited for sending and receiving emails that require special attention to privacy and the person whom you are contacting knows not to include any confidential information. Because the FBI can access emails and other online usage information without a warrant, it is important to use tools that simply keep you anonymous, even if your Internet service provider (ISP) is issued a subpoena to let the cat out of the bag.

The program is called Tor. Tor is a browser bundle that is specifically designed to hide the informational details about the person using it. Most importantly, it creates an anonymous atmosphere by bouncing the origination of your information through a very large, complicated network. The technology of Tor was originally designed by naval intelligence and is used by journalists and whistleblowers. Not only is this another fantastic way of keeping your information anonymous to hackers (see chapter 17), but this can keep the big watchers off your back as well.

The second part with keeping your emails anonymous is to use online messaging services such as SilentSender.com or Hushmail.com. These services do work quite well, but unfortunately they only send from anonymous sources. The email addresses may be anonymous, but your IP address will be traceable. However, using this in combination with Tor will mean that you will be communicating over anonymous email addresses from anonymous destinations.

The key here is to never sign on to any of these accounts without Tor, because if you do, your IP will pop up and be recorded as having signed on at one time. It would not take long for them to conclude that your IP address is obviously associated with the person who created the account in the first place. Once this happens, you've effectively blown your attempt at privacy. In addition, you will have to use pseudonyms (or no names at all) in any contact. While the destinations of the sender and receiver may be anonymous, the email itself is not encrypted, meaning that the content of these emails can be analyzed. If any names are mentioned, they've got you.

One of the interesting perks about using Tor is the fact that they also have apps for smartphones, which means that you will be able to surf and use your anonymous email account while you are mobile.

The only real downfall of Tor is the fact that you cannot really conduct any daily business online—anything that has your current, non-anonymous information. For instance, logging into your online bank account would be useless, since it is steadfastly attached to your own identity.

Interestingly enough, you may technically be able to use social networking utilities through Tor since social networking's entire purpose is connecting with associates through a name by which you are already known, though doing so may be somewhat self-defeating. If anything, it is best to designate which parts of your life you are comfortable and uncomfortable with being watched. For instance, you probably don't need to be concerned about being monitored when purchasing a Beatles vinyl album on eBay, but when doing research on which firearm purchase you are considering, employing privacy methods would be smart.

This is why it is a smart call to only use programs and services that keep you anonymous when there is something you absolutely need to hide. For everything else, keep it open and don't worry about it. Frankly, the watchers probably won't care, and they will simply write it off as noise. In addition, it will add to the perception that you a normal person and increase your chances of not being flagged for analysis.

This is also why you need to be very careful what you say on social networking utilities. Even these days, people are seeing jail time for the opinions they express on sites like Facebook. While Facebook may be an excellent political soapbox, it is our view that times are changing, and perhaps it may be better to keep these things off extensively monitored SNUs in order to maintain a small profile. This is a matter of personal conviction of course, and we are not suggesting that you must keep quiet. However, we are saying that you should be prepared for the worst when posting pictures, opinions, etc., on social networking utilities.

There really is no way to keep the watchers at bay when using SNUs. Ultimately, it comes down to what you don't put on them that matters.

Of course, not all forms of communication are created equally. We now know that the U.S. government is actively storing our text messages and phone call information. When using cell phones, it is very difficult to attain any level of anonymity. However, it is possible to a certain extent.

For instance, the average person can, in fact, purchase a prepaid mobile phone without giving away any information as to who is using the phone. Essentially, all you need to do is purchase a prepaid phone at a store with some kind of subtle facial obstruction for security cameras (hat, fake glasses, etc.), and only pay cash for the phone itself and the minutes. When registering the phone, simply use completely false, random information. Keep in mind, this window may be closing soon, as there are rumors that prepaid phones may require identification in order to purchase them. This is not the case now, but the time may soon be coming.

However, if you intend to keep this phone anonymous, never leave the battery in the phone when it is at your place of residence or business. They can easily pick up the phone through GPS tracking, meaning that the very location of the phone will betray your anonymity, as they most certainly have your address. Taking out the battery will disable the power source, and the phone itself will not physically be able to transmit data, a GPS signal, or even be used as a listening device if they wanted to remotely activate the microphone.

In addition, never text or say anything that may be used to identify you or the person to whom you are communicating on your second phone. This information is not encrypted, and the wireless service you are using is not made to be anonymous. Bear in mind, the wireless service would gladly give up your information in order to avoid a fight with the feds.

If you don't mind spending the money, you can actually purchase pouches that can literally block all wireless signals going to and from your mobile device for about $90. Of course, while constructing a tinfoil pouch from the roll in the kitchen drawer might get you part of the way there, it usually requires a series of metal linings to block out wireless, cellular, and GPS signals (hence, the price tag). This may be an effective option if you are running on an iPhone or Android, which may not allow you to remove the battery. These pouches may also come in handy as a permanent carrying case for your secondary prepaid phone. Also, this is another great way to keep hackers at bay (again, see chapter 17).

Last, don't lose faith in the more conventional methods of communication and doing business. The seemingly lost art of talking face-to-face is perhaps the best possible way to keep from being monitored. Of course, if you are deeply concerned about ears on your conversation, make sure that you and the people with whom you are talking remove the batteries from your phones, place them in a blocker pouch, or simply leave your phones somewhere safe, but somewhere else.

In terms of the conventional methods, you might also consider simply writing or typing out a letter and sending it via snail mail. However, there have been recent reports that the U.S. Postal Service has been scanning the outsides of millions of letters. In fact, some have likened the current USPS surveillance program to the NSA programs, about which were leaked by Edward Snowden. It is unknown exactly how many of our letters have been scanned, and they aren't telling how long they keep the scans. Thus, it should be safe to assume that, if you are corresponding through letters, they know the content of the metadata on the outside: names, addresses, frequency of correspondence, etc.

The only real way around this issue is to send letters from false return addresses, from public mail drop boxes. Unfortunately, the recipient of your letters may have to receive the mail from several third parties so that his or her address does not keep getting flagged.

One somewhat effective way to ensure that your letter is not read by unfriendly eyes is to write out a disinformation letter in regular ink, then on top of it, write out the actual letter in UV ink (which can only be read under a fluorescent or black light). This may give you a slight upper hand in possibly throwing the watchers off your trail. However, in the event that the authorities open your letter, there is a very high chance that they will hit it with a black light, thereby divulging all of the letter's secrets. Don't count on this method as foolproof, but only an added protection.

Nevertheless, if you continue to use several addresses through which you communicate via mail, then you should be able to keep your profile small enough to go unnoticed.

The methods discussed in stage one and two are great for reducing your profile to being almost unnoticeable, especially if you conduct other parts of life in the open. It is always best to appear normal and uninteresting, rather than appearing as if you have something to hide.

However, in the next chapter, we will discuss how to disappear in the event that our current form of government is no longer in existence. The reason why we have designated this stage three is for the simple fact that these methods are a form of insurance against the ultimate threat. In the same way that many minorities could have saved themselves from the Nazis in 1930s Germany through reading the signs and preparing ahead of time, perhaps we should consider our options at this point. Perhaps we should learn how not to draw attention to ourselves, and even if attention is upon us, be extremely difficult to find.

Chapter 19

HERE AT THE END OF IT ALL

And so, the American people are finally drawn away to pay the piper. The flag goes up. It hits the fan. It is finally the end of America…as we know it. With whatever figure of speech you would like to use, this chapter concerns the most likely issues we will have to face and discusses how to face them.

Bear in mind, some of the information in this chapter may be thought of as illegal, evasive, and even somewhat traitorous. However, these tactics are not meant for use in this current age of American history but instead, they are meant for the times when the U.S. has effectively suspended and abandoned her Constitution. It is for a time when the government has broken its word, thereby nullifying our requirement to keep ours. In addition, these are defensive tactics and never to be used for offensive purposes. Essentially, the reason why chapter 19 consists of a grand third stage is because this chapter is your ultimate insurance in the event of a total privacy takeover.

In the same way stage three has always been in place for when identity theft affects your life, stage three, in this sense, is for when government invasion of privacy has already attempted to affect your life.

I emphasize, do not attempt to evade the law with the tactics that are discussed in this chapter. Rather, it is your imperative to live a law-abiding life, and when all else fails, you will have these tactics at your disposal.

MONEY—WHERE IT ALL STARTS

History has shown us that one of the first moves a tyrannical government will make is to confiscate the property and money of the demographics of which they are opposed or whoever attempts to oppose them (WWII era Germany). So, if the U.S. government already sees you as a possible dissenter, or you fall under their demographics list of undesirables, then your wealth and property may be subject to restriction or outright confiscation.

In addition, a tyrannical government is certainly going to restrict the economic capabilities of the persecuted class. For instance, their goal is a cashless society and implementing this form of currency through an embedded chip is under constant discussion by the power elite. This has been a highly coveted goal for the better part of a century, because it affords them a very easy avenue for implementing complete control over society.

If someone is seen to be a dissenter, terrorist, or whoever the powers-that-be deem to be a danger, then all they need to do is turn off the chip. In that case, it is back to the bartering system for the individual or they will starve.

Of course, it may take quite a while to reach this point (not to mention a very large, devastating catalyst or pretext), however, the attempt to monitor and control transactions is already underway. After 9/11, the U.S. put into place the draconian Patriot Act, but few realized the extent of the measures the act contained.

Many saw the Patriot Act as a way of crafting a route to implement martial law in America. While it did certainly consolidate and increase the power of the bureaucracies under the Executive branch, its primary and most overlooked purpose was to tighten controls over money and banking.

In previous years, it was rather easy to find safe havens for our money, even being able to use our own funding in the U.S. with very few forms of identification. Now, it is nearly impossible to live without identification, as it is required in order to open a checking account, and it requires a checking account in order to pay most of our bills that make life in society possible.

One of the main reasons why governments will restrict the transaction capabilities of the persecuted class is because this will inevitably restrict their movements and their ability to evade detainment. For example, U.S. agencies and cooperating governments froze the accounts of anyone considered to be a terrorist.

Restrict money and you've restricted capabilities. This is why it is important for individuals to invest in the ability to maintain their economic capabilities in the unfortunate event of a tyrannical takeover.

One of the best ways to accomplish this is by investing in precious metals: silver in particular. Precious metals, from the beginnings of recorded history, have always been worth something. Thus, if the powers-that-be attempt to restrict your ability to survive by restricting your money, you will still have a way of purchasing life's necessities. In addition, this will allow you to avoid leaving a paper trail.

The reason why we suggest silver rather than gold is because silver is easier to trade. It is far simpler to barter one troy ounce of silver for a bag of groceries than to purchase half the grocery store with bar of gold. Silver is considered by the prepared as the key to continuing life after some kind of economic collapse or tyranny. With enough silver saved up, you could cultivate connections, buy food, and even make larger purchases, all while maintaining a high level of untraceable privacy.

However, even the U.S. government has criminally confiscated precious metals from the hands of private citizens. This is why it is important that you have a place to hide it in the event that the government attempts to do so again. It is preferable that you store your stash of silver on an off-site property, away from your own residence, and preferably not with precious metal investment companies. If the government intends to confiscate precious metals, these companies will be the first doors on which they knock.

Make sure your silver is locked away, secure, hidden, and safe. Never speak of it with anyone. That stash is your safety net and refuge, and you would never want to compromise it.

Even in the event that the U.S. government attempts to convert the U.S. economy to a cashless society, folks will have little problem with cutting a backroom deal when you approach them with silver.

However, especially during tough times, diversification is essential. Offshore banking has become very popular these days, especially since taxes appear to be steadily increasing with little sign of stopping. Keep in mind that we are not suggesting the use of offshore banking as way to evade taxes. Though some successfully accomplish this, we do feel as if it is proper to "give Caesar what is Caesar's," and it also costs a pretty penny for the legal advice to accomplish this successfully.

However, offshore banking can offer a way to keep your money in a place that is not under IRS jurisdiction, is a non-Tax Information Exchange Agreement (TIEA) country, and is not a member of the European Union. Using a bank that does not cooperate with U.S. banking law is important, because they will not give out the name of the account holder, allowing you to operate in a cashless society with anonymity. Unfortunately, it would be difficult to give out the names of banks and countries that would work for this purpose because that list changes on a monthly basis. Simply research non-TIEA banks and you will soon find a list of possibilities.

One of the best parts about working with non-TIEA countries is the fact that you can even set up private dummy corporations of your own within them. These corporations are advantageous, as the government of the foreign country won't even know the name of the person controlling it. (Arguably, the reason why they do this is because this attracts business from wealthy, but privacy-minded people.) Thus, you can set up a bank account in the name of your corporation, and even if the country's government is asked by the U.S. to divulge the name of the account holder, they simple wouldn't have the information to do so. You could even use this dummy corporation to operate within the U.S.—buying land, vehicles, paying rent, and other activities. Intelligence agencies have been using these methods for years.

In addition, many of these banks will provide you with a debit card, checks, and other ways to pay your bills through the account, and these forms of payment would be valid in the U.S., provided you are operating on U.S. dollars (or whatever currency is valid in the U.S. at the time).

Perhaps the biggest drawback to this tactic is the fact that it usually costs upwards in the thousands of dollars to properly set it up. In addition, it is best if you hire an attorney whose expertise is in the field of helping expatriots (expats). If you have the funds to be able to accomplish this, then we recommend implementing this tactic as soon as possible. Using an offshore dummy corporation bank account is a fantastic way to build up a savings stash for the coming difficult times.

One of the most obvious ways to make transactions is through cash. Even in a cashless society, some will still accept it as a form of payment. A society will likely never go totally cashless, as something is always worth what someone is willing to pay. On the flip side of that coin, something is always worth what someone else will accept for payment. Perhaps the reason why we feel cash is not as good as silver is because cash is subject to inflation. Today the cash in your pocket is worth a bag of groceries, but in an economic environment of hyperinflation, $200 may not even be enough to buy a loaf of bread. Silver, on the other hand, will actually become more valuable during times of economic decline.

LEAVE A NAME BEHIND YOU

Earlier in this book, we discussed how easy it is for identity thieves to latch themselves onto a victim's identification. Utilizing existing identification is very easy, but unfortunately, operating on clean identification comes with a much higher level of difficulty.

The reason is that first world governments are becoming much more efficient at how they issue identification. Moving about inside a hostile country can become extremely difficult without a clean ID, especially if your identification has been flagged. If you run into one, just one checkpoint, it may be over. If your ID does not check out, if it doesn't match your description, or if it even raises suspicion, then you will most likely be detained and investigated. In a world under martial law, ruled by draconian policies, it is important to appear normal at first, and even second glance.

Ultimately, you must implement two essential tactics. The first is to avoid being asked for identification in the first place, thus limiting your chances of running into a bad situation. If you are driving, then know where the checkpoints are located, and obey all traffic laws to the letter. When on foot, do not involve yourself in any complicated situations that may require you to produce an ID (bars, clubs, public events, etc.). Try to get into a routine where you can survive without being asked for identification in your daily interactions.

Using a fake ID may be able to help you to a certain extent. However, if the authorities stop you and they check your identification against any kind of database, then you are in even worse trouble. Be very cautious with fake IDs, as they can betray you even faster than not having identification in the first place. The important part about acquiring a fake ID is to purchase it from overseas. In the U.S., it is illegal to make or own a fake ID (with the exception of novelty purposes, but that means the quality of the ID should have very limited likeness to the real thing). If you want the magnetic strip on the back to work, then you will need to purchase it from overseas or acquire the machines to make your own. Nevertheless, we feel as if it simply isn't worth it, as a fake ID is often more dangerous to you than not having one at all.

If anything, the cheapest route is to avoid being asked for identification and also get to a place where you can accomplish this effectively.

However, there are ways that you can move about with a clean ID. As we mentioned before, it is possible to operate in the U.S. through offshore bank accounts. In the same way, it is possible to move about in the U.S. with international identification that is issued from a foreign country.

This method can be very costly, as you will most likely have to acquire a second citizenship from the foreign country that issued it. Often times, a second citizenship will require you to hire attorneys, buy land in the other country, or even spend a certain amount of time in that country. In addition, just because you have an International Driver's License doesn't necessarily mean that it will work inside the U.S. Since the list of jurisdictions of cooperating countries and laws regarding international driver's licenses are always changing, our advice is to simply seek out an attorney that specializes in this field.

One highly advantageous method you could use is to acquire an international driver's license from the same country in which you are banking through your dummy corporation. Not only will you have wealth in that country, but you would also be considered a lawful resident. If you had to run to that country, you could effectively live there if you had to. Often times, if the banking laws do not cooperate with the U.S., then it may also be a non-extradition country.

Overall, acquiring a second citizenship and a valid international driver's license that will work inside the U.S. (even during a time of martial law) could be the golden goose of tactics. Not only would you be able to operate without being concerned about an identification check, but you could also buy property.

There would effectively be no law or policy to threaten your identification's validity, provided the U.S. hasn't kicked out foreign nationals. Curiously, even if the U.S. has decided to kick out foreign nationals, the U.S. would theoretically deport you back to your other country, precisely where your wealth is already located.

In addition, when applying for an international driver's license or secondary citizenship, you may not even have to use your full name. While you may not necessarily be able to change your name to something different, you may be able to use your middle name as your first name. Essentially, if there were an identification check against your name in the U.S., they wouldn't even come close to knowing who you really are.

Again, seek the appropriate legal advice, as this tactic can become extremely complicated and extremely pricey. Nevertheless, it can be done, as this is another method that has been used by intelligence agencies.

Unfortunately, there is no foolproof, ironclad system of running with a clean identification. While you might be able to dodge and confuse the system today, you may not be able to do so tomorrow. By far, having clean identification is the hardest part about leaving a name behind you and maintaining invisibility. The whole purpose of identification is to identify an individual, labeling him or her, attaching demographics and descriptions, and especially assisting the government in finding persons of interests. This is not necessarily a bad thing these days, but it could be dangerous for persecuted people in the future.

If you are unable to acquire a foreign driver's license or identification card, then it is best if you simply lose your identification and run to an area where you will have the lowest likelihood of being asked for it by the authorities. You may simply have to leave your name behind you, especially if you know for a fact that you are in a persecuted demographic. Even these days, people can go for years without identification, thus this can be a possible tactic for you as well.

Otherwise, it may be worth your while to simply use your own ID. Not every checkpoint will be a situation that will have an official running an identification check against a database. In some cases, they will simply do a quick glance over the ID and move you along, as they may be in search of a single person of interest. In addition, it could be a DUI or drug checkpoint, meaning that they are simply searching for intoxicated drivers. While they may do an identification check, it is likely that they will not.

Nevertheless, it is best to avoid these situations if you can. Identification will unfortunately be the downfall of many when martial law takes effect.

GOING PLACES

Transportation is yet another tricky matter, especially when the government is attempting to restrict travel. During a crisis, interstates and main routes are always very congested to a point where they become impractical and even impossible to traverse. A quick glance at the news during an evacuation from a pending natural disaster will validate this point. Not only will there be a flood of travelers attempting to leave highly populated zones, but government-run checkpoints will exacerbate this problem.

In addition, because of drones, satellites, traffic cameras, and authorities on the ground, your vehicle could be a dead giveaway to who you are. If you are on the run, it is best to simply leave your own primary vehicle behind you, as it is registered in your name. During times of martial law, surveillance will be put into overdrive, and vehicles will come under heightened and targeted scrutiny. They know that you will attempt to leave, so they will set up as many obstacles and eyes on the road as their infrastructure capabilities will allow.

If your resources are limited, one of the best ways to get around in this situation is to use transportation with off-road capabilities. Roads will be monitored, but not all traversable routes will be.

Riding a bicycle may be a great way to move about your area. You would be able to observe and assess situations more thoroughly before you enter into potentially monitored areas, and you would be able to escape quickly if you had to. Of course, bicycles are severely limited in speed and carrying capacity, but for getting from Point A to Point B undetected, there are few better options.

In addition, using an on/off-road motorcycle (Kawasaki KLR 650 for instance), would offer you the ability to quickly escape, even while carrying a hefty amount of supplies or a passenger. The only drawback is the fact that these are registered motor vehicles, meaning that you might be identified. If identified, then it is only a matter of time before the vehicle is found, especially if they have drones or helicopters dispatched in your area of travel. Nevertheless, it is still an excellent option, especially if you need to make a lightning fast escape to safer roads.

However, if you have an international driver's license through a dual citizenship, you should be able to buy a secondary vehicle and register it under your other name. This would give you the ability to drive into monitored zones in your own vehicle and still stay under the radar. This, of course, will cost quite a bit of money and is entirely dependent upon your success with the methods we discussed above.

In addition, especially if you have untracked wealth that has not been confiscated, you could run on taxi services and even utilize a network of drivers who are not at risk for being detained. It is not recommended that you take public transportation, as authorities will regularly stop these. If they are searching for particular demographics and persons of interest, then the authorities will most certainly monitor trains, buses, and subways.

While it may be the slowest option, proceeding on foot may be the best you can do, given your situation. Do keep in mind that even if you move about on foot, eyes in the sky may still track you.

In these situations, it is almost always best to utilize old military tactics when moving from Point A to Point B. Never travel during the day. The only time you should travel is from dusk to dawn. During the failing light is usually the best, especially during periods in the day when light is in rapid transition, as it makes focusing on and identifying a target much more difficult. In addition, the dusk and dawn has been known to throw off surveillance technology. While this may not necessarily be the case for modern surveillance devices used by the U.S., lesser-equipped forces from other UN countries may monitor you. Militaries travel at night because it is harder to track them, and this means that you should too.

WHERE YOU LAY YOUR HEAD

Where you live is one of the most crucial aspects of avoiding the authorities. It is one of the most fundamental parts of living off grid, as your address is perhaps the first place that the authorities will pay a visit (more like show up in black ski masks with sledgehammers, attack dogs, and AR-15s).

When martial law is established, the longer you stay at your current place of residence, the higher the risk. Simply staying home and hoping for the best should not, by any means, be an option. The minority populations tried it in WWII-era Germany and Russia, and it didn't work out so well for them.

The first order of business should be to obtain lodging in a place that is not connected to your name. Whether it is squatting in some run-down house or paying someone rent in an off-the-books transaction, you need to get out immediately.

Living on property owned by someone else is certainly a good option. However, you need to make sure that the taxes, utility bills, and other services are paid in someone else's name and that you are able to pay them in silver or cash. In addition, you need to be sure that he or she is trustworthy (close family or friend) and also not on the list of arrest-worthy demographics.

Squatting is also an option, though it is vital that you maintain a low profile while doing so. By definition, squatting is illegal, meaning that if your new residence is discovered, you may be subject to scrutiny by the same people you were running from in the first place. If you do end up squatting, do so in an area that is too rural to patrol regularly, or make sure that there are so many other squatters, that you will be lost in the confusion when the authorities get there.

These, of course, are very low-level methods of evading detection and are considered rather risky, dangerous, and may result in a primitive standard of living. If you can, utilizing the methods below should keep the authorities from finding where you live, especially if you are implementing the methods we discussed above.

First, if you were able to set up an offshore dummy corporation, then you can actually buy land in the U.S. through it. It may be a little more difficult to do than a private purchase and again, you may need to hire an attorney to facilitate the purchase. However, foreign corporations accomplish this on a regular basis. Your name will not show up on the paperwork and even if the U.S. government inquired of the foreign nation to find out who owns the corporation, their government wouldn't be able to say because even they don't know. Essentially, you are living on this property and no one has any idea who owns it. You could even pay the property taxes and utility bills through your corporation, meaning that your name never shows up on any paperwork.

Second, a great way to keep your name from showing up on a deed is by setting up a land trust. Again, you will need to hire an attorney to do so, but it is basically setting up a non-entity (like a corporation) to take ownership of the property. Often times, major corporations will do this in order to hide the fact that they may be buying up large chunks of land. However, if the authorities issued a warrant to your attorney, the information of who controls the land will show up on the paperwork. This option is effective, but not ironclad.

It is very important that your information never shows up on any taxes or bills. Never accidentally pay them with your own checking account, as this will certainly draw attention and lead them back to you. Always pay the bills on your retreat property through your foreign corporation or land trust.

Also, never talk to anyone about these properties, especially to folks you may not be able to trust. Having an untracked patch of land to which you can go may not be as valuable today, but during martial law and mass unrest, people have killed for that kind of property. Keep these things a tightly guarded secret.

THOSE NEAR AND DEAR

Understand that no man is an island. If you attempt to take on this gargantuan task of running off grid yourself, it is likely that you may fail. It is absolutely essential to have folks you can trust. Through them, you will likely be able to do the following:

- Find lodging

- Find work

- Find food

- Access transportation

- Live through third parties and surrogates

- Send communications

- Store valuables

There really are no criteria for determining who is trustworthy and who is not. Sometimes you simply have to trust your gut instincts. However, going it alone will place 100 percent of the burden on you and on those in your care in a newly hostile world. Looking back through history, it is clear that many survivors of genocide and persecution were able to make it out alive because of good people who helped them.

Be sure to utilize your existing networks. Your church, your workplace, your clubs, your old war buddies, or whatever tight-knit group of which you are a part can be highly useful during these times.

In addition, it is possible to forge business relationships, especially if you are able to run on silver, cash, or offshore funding. If you still have access to your wealth, then you can often barter, buy, and negotiate your way into living off the books.

Keeping your wealth intact and accessible is perhaps the most important way to forge business relationships and keep acquiring resources to survive.

Never underestimate the power of human connections and friendship during times of turmoil.

Chapter 20

LEARNING TO OUT-SMART THE BEAST: A LOOK AT STRATEGY

We have discussed at length about what information identity thieves are after, and we have also talked about how they can use your personal data for their benefit. However, we have not gone into depth about who identity thieves are. It is important to understand the nature of a thief when considering your strategy, as thinking like a thief can offer brilliant insight. Bear in mind that in order to do this, one must make grandiose, sweeping generalizations. We understand that not all thieves are created equally, and some thieves will be very different from the profile we will provide below. Nevertheless, this is a valuable exercise, as it requires making assumptions in order to prepare for a hypothetical event.

PROFILE OF AN IDENTITY THIEF

Identity thieves, in general, tend to possess somewhat higher intelligence, depending on what they are after and why they are attempting to take down targets. In general, motivation has perhaps the most prominent effect on the competency of a thief.

If the thief is simply trying to steal for money to buy drugs (which is often the case in impoverished and densely populated areas), the thief will be more direct and random. Along the same lines, thieves who steal because of poverty or to settle a debt tend to inflict the smallest damage, leave the most evidence, and eventually end up behind bars. This type of thief tends to possess the least, but most annoying, threat value. Often, a desperation–motivated theft is devoid of method, reason, and effective tactics.

Usually, identity theft is not spawned from desperation. Because of the nature of sophistication, higher level of mental difficulty and planning, and the requirement of intelligence concerning understanding human psychology, utilizing technology, and even evading law enforcement, an identity thief often gets into the business for the large, but easy, financial payoff. In addition, the thrill of power is very attractive.

It is not usually out of desperation that identity thieves begin perfecting their craft. It often has to do with ego, the feeling of competence, and the astonishingly low level of risk.

Indeed, identity thieves are excellent at assessing risk. It is why they are identity thieves and not conventional thieves. In most cases, conventional theft requires the criminal to actually be present to commit the crime, dramatically elevating the level of risk. Identity thieves love the fact that they can commit their crime without ever having to approach the crime scene and sometimes perpetrate the identity theft from thousands of miles away. Also, identity thieves will most likely never have to face their victims and can easily dodge the threat of law enforcement through technological means and sly tactics. In many schemes, they can simply carry out their deeds from behind their computer screens, sipping on cappuccinos from the comfort of their local coffee shops.

Simply put, identity thieves want to steal, but they want the smallest possible chance of getting caught, the largest possible chance of success, and the least possible amount of work. This is why most identity thieves will attempt to filter out the hard targets and only go after the easy ones. The harder the target, the more risk and work are involved.

However, identity thieves often love a challenge. They know that sometimes the harder the challenge, the greater the financial benefit. For instance, a CEO of a large corporation may have excellent protections in place against identity theft, but an identity thief may choose to attack regardless because success would mean extracting a very fat paycheck from the victim.

The reason why identity thieves are usually not desperate per se is because successful operations will require planning, time, funding, and energy. Someone desperate would not have the resources to accomplish this. Also, in most cases, identity theft is not a crime of passion. Identity thieves are usually business-minded individuals who are more concerned with the financial benefit. While they do enjoy the feeling of power, effectiveness, and out-smarting their targets and law enforcement…they would most likely not take on the task if it were not for the payoff.

This is why it is important not to underestimate identity thieves. They are highly intelligent risk assessors, and they often thrive off of the puzzle, the mind-game of exploiting a crack in a wall and slipping in unnoticed.

Also, bear in mind that an identity thief could be anyone, including someone you know personally and to whom you may be very closely associated. According to the Baltimore Sun, a report on April 25, 2011 stated:

If your identity is stolen, there's a good chance you know the thief.

One out of seven cases of identity theft last year involved a relative, roommate, co-worker or some other acquaintance, according to an annual survey by California-based Javelin Strategy & Research. While ID theft overall fell 28 percent last year, "friendly fraud" experienced a slight increase, Javelin reports.

This means that you have a one-in-seven chance of personally knowing the identity thief. Also, keep in mind that this statistic was created based only on the cases where they were able to ascertain the origin of the identity theft. There could be more, and that statistic could be even higher.

This is why it is absolutely critical to your strategy that you trust only those who absolutely need to possess your personal information. It is also important to understand that identity theft can be perpetrated by someone who is highly competent, good at understanding and avoiding risk, audacious enough to perpetrate the crime, and smart enough to get away with it. Make sure that your circle, the people who know your personal information, stays small. If identity theft does occur within this circle, then the smaller it is, the easier it will be to track down the origin of the leak.

THINKING LIKE A TYRANT

Because we've already discussed the most basic elements of a tyrannical government at length in the beginning chapters of this book, we don't need to spend too much time on profiling a privacy-invading government. However, there are a few points to review in order to help you prepare your strategy.

First and foremost, while identity thieves are highly intelligent, audacious, and thirsty for the feeling of power, the government is the same way—but multiplied exponentially. If you want to find the most efficient minds who know exactly how to track, trace, and profile the law-abiding citizen, look no further than the federal government and data mining corporations.

They are very good at extracting your personal data. But, in the same way that the identity thief needs to spend time learning about his or her target before the attack, government is doing the exact same thing. Remember: the spies go before the army.

One of the most important things to understand about a snooping government is that they will ardently claim that they aren't spying while they are continually applying enormous resources and efforts to carry out their spying programs. Despite whatever they may claim or whatever rationalizations they will give the citizenry, understand that tracking you is, and always will be, their prime objective.

They have billions of dollars to accomplish this purpose, they have the technology to carry it out, and they have the will to see it through. Their aim is to construct comprehensive and current profiles on every single resident of the U.S., while also continuing their surveillance programs and monitoring the public on a constant and ongoing basis. They simply want to know you—all of you. They don't want just the basics; they want to know who you are to the core and to know what you are going to do before you do it.

However, they seek to accomplish this objective through mostly technological means. While past tyrants have used their boots on the ground and secret informants, they have long realized that technology is the key for surveillance in the twenty-first century. Of course, nearly all identity thieves think this way, and the federal government is not exempt from this categorization.

They know that the best way to spy on an entire society is to manipulate them into accepting the surveillance. All they have to do is get people hooked and dependent on technology. Once this occurs, they can use this technology for their surveillance pleasure. The only way to keep from being watched is to avoid technology, but in this era, that is not easily accomplished.

While it is certainly possible to confuse the watchers through tools that provide cover and anonymity while using technology, this often costs too much and is too complicated for the average citizen. In addition, these methods may not confuse the watchers for very long. If they are seeking a specific target, then it really is only a matter of time before their target is located.

Nevertheless, the watchers are not omniscient. While they do have mountains of resources available to them, it is possible to avoid their gaze. They can be deceived, but unfortunately, it is very difficult to do so. It is usually in anonymity, maintaining a small profile, and becoming a more difficult target to track that are how the privacy-minded individuals can keep from popping up on their screens. Their ability to track you down depends on their logistical resources, meaning that the smaller your profile is, the easier it is for you to "get lost" in the seas of other folks they are currently tracking.

The watchers are powerful, but they are not all powerful. Keeping this in mind will be the key to crafting your privacy strategy.

YOUR STRATEGY—WALK BEFORE YOU RUN

In *Underground Privacy Secrets,* we have discussed absolutely horrific scenarios where Big Brother takes hold of our last vestiges of liberty…and squeezes. In addition, we've also talked about the horrors of identity theft and how it can come into your life and rip your credit and your reputation to shreds.

However, sometimes when we come into contact with these kinds of fears and it suddenly strikes a place within us that we simply cannot ignore, that is when we are inspired to implement a change in lifestyle. In making a sudden transition from sleeping to awake, there can often be an uncomfortable and sudden jolt. It usually isn't until we experience a paradigm shift, that we undertake the task of implementing serious changes.

Many of us tend to drop everything and make these changes very quickly. Others implement the lifestyle changes rather slowly. The key is to only make these changes as your time and funding allow. While the most common mistake is to let this information sink in and do nothing, it is another mistake to take this information and make illogically quick decisions, overstretching your capabilities to adapt financially.

In this chapter, we will not explore what changes to make, but rather discuss how to make the switch. Becoming a privacy-minded individual is important, but not at a higher expense than you are able to pay.

One of the best ways to approach your strategy is to first assess the most imminent threats and then second, assess your resources and capabilities. Tackling the task of protecting yourself from identity theft should be methodic in nature. This way you are sure to keep from accidentally leaving yourself open, setting up your defenses to be comprehensive and complete. Basing your strategy on the balance between your threats and resources will ensure that you don't overstretch yourself, while ensuring that you take on patching the largest gaps in your defenses first.

Bearing this in mind, we can move forward knowing that we aren't missing the most important parts, while also perfecting your strategy in a financially feasible manner.

THREAT VERSUS RESOURCES

The threat versus resources balance will allow you to defend yourself to the best of your strategic and financial capabilities. For instance, if your funds are limited, don't try to take on Big Brother while you are still leaving your back door open to common identity theft. In many ways, taking care of one threat often kills two birds with one stone. In addition, there are plenty of inexpensive (even free) ways to protect yourself before you start spending money on the comprehensive, but higher-costing methods.

Ultimately, what we are trying to cover in this chapter is to make sure that you do not overstretch your capabilities to the point where you burn out and give up.

However, one very interesting aspect about the threat versus resources principle is the fact that the more resources you have, the more dangerous and numerous are your threats. Also, the fewer resources you have, the less dangerous and numerous the threats. For example, if you are very wealthy, then there is a good chance that you may be a target for identity theft. However, you have the financial resources to pay for adequate protection. If you are barely scraping by and living paycheck to paycheck, then you won't have the money for comprehensive identity theft protection. But then again, you're probably not a major target.

We are going to guide you on how to make the lifestyle transition to accomplishing your own Invisibility Objective. We understand that our readers have varying levels of preparedness and varying levels of resources. So, if you have several methods already accomplished, simply check them off and move on. We'll start from the beginning—a very good place to start.

A LITTLE INITIAL SECURITY FOR FREE

Let us say, for instance, that you have absolutely no preparedness against identity theft or government privacy intrusion—whatsoever. One of the very first things you should do is to identify and address the threats that are most likely going to occur in your life. The issue here is not necessarily guarding against hypothetical threats (government surveillance), but to address the threats with the highest likelihood of occurring in your life. We want to figure out where the possible information leaks are occurring and stop them.

In most cases, your only costs here will be time and energy. If you have all kinds of papers, credit cards, and other official documentation such as bills, insurance policies, and tax documents scattered about, then it's time to gather them all up.

We did suggest that you would need to get lock boxes and safes, but for now, simply get your papers together and organize them. The more organized you are, the less likely you will end up losing an important document. Lost documents can end up in the wrong hands, so make sure you've located every single sheet of paper that can be used against you.

Next, you should find good places to hide your important documents. It is crucial that you do not pick one single place to store every single document you own, because if that stash is found, then the individual involved in the theft will effectively make off with your entire identity. As we mentioned before, this is basically Stage Two in building your identity theft protection labyrinth. Separate your documents into categories (such as insurance, banking, credit, and tax document categories), and then hide them in secure places. A smart practice would be to hide them in places that are unseen from someone standing on the ground. If you have a top shelf in a closet, then hide your documents there: a thief would have to grab a stool or a chair in order to even see the stash. Adding as many steps between the documents being located and the documents being stolen is a great approach to making the identity theft more difficult to a potential thief.

You should also hide these documents in such a way that it doesn't even appear that documents would be kept in that location. For instance, rather than hiding them in an obvious document case, hide them instead in an unmarked box along with old holiday cards and miscellaneous clothing items. Even better would be to mark the box, "holiday trinkets" or something along those lines. Use any means in order to throw off a possible identity thief, and feel free to get creative. For more ideas on hideaway caches, check out Solutions From Science's book, How to Hide Your Guns. The suggestions are for more than weapons caches.

However, in using these methods, it is possible to lose entire categories of documentation, which is also going to be a rather annoying headache. You may want to write down where these categories of documentation are located and be sure that you keep this paper in a very secure location that requires a key in order to access it. One great way to ensure that your documentation can be found by you (but not by others) is to create an easy encryption of your separate categories, and write them down on a piece of paper.

For example: for car insurance in the coat closet, you can simply write down something like: CI -> Holiday Trinkets In Coats. If you keep this paper in the glove box of your car, then the thief must have your car key in order to locate these documents, know where to look inside the car, and then decipher the meaning of "CI" and "Holiday Trinkets In Coats". To you, it's an easy way to remember the location, but to a thief, it would be out of context. It would take even longer to figure it out, placing more time and energies between the thief and the target. In addition, a thief who targets your vehicle is most likely after your cup holder change and wouldn't have any idea what the paper means.

As we stated above, not all thieves are after the same exact targets. Thieves who break into vehicles are usually in search of loose change and are after your stereo. The target isn't that useless piece of paper in the glove box, meaning that it will most likely be left undisturbed. Also, they will most likely break into cars and not houses.

An identity thief, even one on the inside (family member, friend, roommate, etc.), wouldn't think to check a glove box for directions on where to look for your documentation. They would check your office desk, kitchen drawers, and any other obvious location, most likely giving up if he or she didn't find it within a few hours. In addition, identity thieves would rather not break into vehicles. They are tricky to get into, and breaking into cars would have a higher risk of getting caught in the act. Identity thieves despise high-risk situations.

PROTECTING YOUR TECH

The second step in your strategy needs to answer the protection of your technology, your online accounts, and your mobile devices. We are also including your credit cards and bank accounts in this, as they have a higher likelihood of being accessed online rather than being accessed through theft of paperwork.

Of course, we aren't saying that protecting these parts of your identity is of less importance than consolidating and hiding your physical documents. However, we do feel as if you should accomplish the tasks in the above section first, as this can be done in an afternoon or a weekend, and it will not cost you a penny.

To protect your devices, it is important that you immediately begin to protect your home network, especially if your home network is broadcasting a wireless signal. We discussed how to do this in previous chapters (see chapter 17).

The reason why this should be your first step is that it should not cost you anything, and this can be done rather quickly. For information on how to do this with your home network, simply give the manufacturer of your router a call, or you can also find tutorials online. Again, this should not take you much longer than an afternoon or weekend to accomplish the task.

Next, because most operating systems have basic free firewalls, you should go through the setup process and make it operational. From this point, only highly accomplished hackers would be able to crack your system protections on your home network. The reason why we suggest that this should be your first step in terms of securing your technological devices is because the next step is to secure your usernames and passwords to your various accounts. If you did not secure your home network, then a hacker may be able to extract them by remotely spying on your unprotected system.

The next thing you should do is to retrieve all of your passwords and usernames to your accounts. If you don't know a password or username, most businesses that run online accounts have a retrieve password or forgot password link that will take you through the appropriate steps to retrieve your information. The usernames and passwords you retrieve should be everything from online banking accounts to email addresses to the password to your laptop.

Next, you should go ahead and change your passwords. It is always smart to get into the practice of changing your passwords regularly, so this can be your first of many password rotations. Also, be sure to write down these usernames and passwords, as this would be next to impossible to remember. DO NOT use the same password (or similar passwords) to all of your accounts, as this is just asking for problems.

Because of the importance of this piece of paper, we feel as if it should be on you at all times, rarely ever leaving your side. We recommend keeping it in your purse or wallet.

NOTE: Interestingly, there is one particular username and password that you should not write down, and that is the account information to your identity theft protection company. We will discuss why in the next section.

Your next step concerns your mobile devices. Yes, you should have already changed the username and password (PIN) on your mobile devices, but it is now time to go through your smartphone, tablet, iPhone, iPod Touch, iPad, or any other electronic device and remove any applications that you don't need. Pay special attention to the application install requests that you received from emails, marketing campaigns, texts, etc. We feel as if it is simply best if you do not use applications that aren't considered official, or if you were prompted to download them from an outside party. The reason is what we discussed in chapter 12, in how hackers can access your mobile device remotely through a phishing application that they were able to bait you into installing.

After that, you should beef up the security measures on your device, and simply do not install any foreign or suspicious applications in the future. If you are prompted by an outside party to install an application onto your device, only do so if you absolutely have to.

Your next step is to begin clamping down on your Internet security gaps. Be sure to make it harder to save cookies on to your browser. If there are certain sites that you trust (which is a legitimate concern), then feel free to select those sites as exemptions. They should be able to save cookies to your browser, making it a bit easier to use the site in the future. Also, some browsers have better security options than others. Go through the additional security features and work with the options you like. Of course, the strength of your security is up to your own discretion, as the tighter your security measures, the more inconvenient your surfing experience will be. Nevertheless, bear in mind that the browser is one of your weakest points in terms of your technological security.

Assuming you've already changed your password information for your social networking utilities, now is the time to address how much information you should actually be posting on your profile. Especially in terms of Facebook, it is not smart for you to have a totally public profile (unless you are using the Facebook account for networking/marketing purposes). In addition, do not have your place of birth, your full name, or your date of birth posted on the "About" section of your profile. You should then go through your photos and delete anything that might place a gap in your identity security. Again, this is up to your own discretion. Also, do not post any other dates, and it is best if you remove your past and present employers and specific addresses. You may not want to remove past or present schools or colleges, but do understand that this information may also be used against you.

Since you are now on your social networking utility account, this is a fantastic time to beef up your privacy measures on there as well. Again, this is up to your discretion.

One type of application that you should certainly download is an anti-theft protection app. As we mentioned in chapter 17, they can locate and protect your devices in the event of a theft. These are highly useful tools, and in most cases, they are free for up to a certain number of devices.

YOUR FIRST PURCHASES

One you get to this point, you now have the money saved up to make a few purchases towards your security. This is an incredibly wise investment, especially considering how this is an opportunity to invest in the prevention of identity theft and even in insuring against the possibility of it actually occurring in your life.

The absolute first thing you need to do is invest in an identity theft protection company. Usually, it is a monthly or yearly subscription, and it shouldn't cost you more than $25 a month at the most for the most comprehensive coverage. For basic, but still rather adequate coverage, you're most likely looking at $10 per month. Not only will they offer insurance against your damages in the event of identity theft taking place, but they will also monitor your identity to make sure that no one unauthorized is using your SSN, credit cards, bank accounts, etc. This is an excellent second line of defense because, even if the identity thieves get through your first line, the identity theft protection company is there to ensure that they don't get away with it.

This is also the reason why we said to keep your passwords in your purse or wallet. Companies like LifeLock offer stolen wallet protection, meaning that if your wallet is stolen, they will shut down and track the accounts associated with the contents of the wallet. Thus, even if your purse or wallet is taken right before your eyes, you merely need to give your company a call, and they will get busy staving off disaster. This adds a double-layer of protection for your passwords: they are harder to steal since your wallet or purse is always near you, and even if the thief succeeds, you've already ensured that your accounts are protected.

Next, you should invest in purchasing a more comprehensive firewall system for your home network. While most basic firewalls that come installed on computers are relatively strong, hackers can often break them in a matter of time. Purchasing a good firewall system will ensure that you can keep 95 percent of even very good hackers at bay.

Next, you should look after your physical documentation, so it's back to your closets full of paperwork.

Unfortunately, good hiding spots won't keep out everyone. It may do the job for a certain amount of time, but it is obvious that the best way to keep your paperwork safe is to lock it up.

Of course, this is one of those situations where the kind of lock box or safe you buy is entirely dependent upon your resources at the time. For instance, you would not want to go out and buy a $1000 safe when you can only afford a $35 lock box. Again it is the threat versus resources balance that we want to stress.

If you can only afford inexpensive lock boxes, then you will need to understand that you should probably buy one for each category you are protecting. Unfortunately, lock boxes do not offer a very high level of protection, as most of those locks are rather easy for even a novice to pick. This means that you should still keep your boxes in separate caches. Where the delicacy of balance comes in, is the principle that, if you have $200 to spend on lock boxes, but you can buy a sturdy safe for that amount, then it is often best to err on the side of security. Spend the money on the safe. As time goes on, and you feel you can get a better safe, then feel free to do so.

If you are able to acquire a good safe, then you don't really need to worry about keeping your documents separate, as the safe can now act as a far more effective labyrinth. At this point, you don't need the encoded piece of paper in your glove box, as now you only need to remember one combination. However, we do not recommend writing down the combination if at all possible. That number is certainly something you should keep only in your head.

WHAT ABOUT GOVERNMENT PRIVACY CONCERNS?

This should get you started on your road to protecting yourself from identity theft. In the next chapter, we will discuss how best to begin addressing your privacy concerns. We wanted to discuss identity theft first, as we feel it is a more imminent threat. However, we do feel as if privacy concerns are becoming more serious with every news story about the watchers.

Since we have finished addressing the best strategies for implementing your identity theft protection measures, it is now time for us to address how to avoid being seen in our surveillance nightmare. It is these strategies that have the potential to cost a large chunk of money, but in return you will get cover, concealment, security, and the ultimate insurance. The goal here is to make sure that your name changes while your standard of living and your freedom change very little.

Chapter 21

IMPLEMENTING YOUR ANTI-SURVEILLANCE STRATEGY & ADDITIONAL PROTECTIONS

As we said in the last chapter, you can kill two birds with one stone by implementing your identity theft protections first before you start on your anti-surveillance strategy. It is much harder to track down and watch someone who is already covering his or her tracks.

The biggest aspect to understand about covering your tracks against government surveillance is the fact that the smaller your profile is, the less chance you will be noticed. As we discovered during the summer of 2013, the NSA is currently constructing comprehensive profiles on every American.

While this sounds absolutely horrifying, bear in mind that there are over 300 million Americans in the U.S. This means that they are trying to build these comprehensive profiles and trying to track a massive amount of people all at the same time. While they do have the technology at their disposal to do so, they are doing this through the technology we use. If you were to simply stop using technology (or use it less), then it is going to be very difficult for them to read your footprints—as compared to the rest of Americans.

Disappearing in the sea of data is the best way to lessen how much attention and time they will spend on you. Anonymity is easily achieved when there are lots and lots of other people under surveillance. It is very possible to disappear and not be watched. In addition, as we said before, it is possible to confuse the system by filtering your identity through other jurisdictions, utilizing private means of communication, and even weaving your communication and dealings through a series of networks.

Nevertheless, it is important to note that you are going to be tracked by four basic categories of data: eyes, location, transaction, and communication. If you can knock out all four of these categories with whatever you are doing, then you can evade them.

TAKING YOUR FIRST STEPS

Again, we do not want you to overstretch your energies or financial ability in combating government privacy intrusion. Essentially, it is always best to begin the free and inexpensive strategies before you begin implementing the more costly ones.

While identity theft protection has more to do with time and energy, anti-surveillance and off-grid living tend to rack up quite the price tag. However, the more you spend, usually the better protection you will receive.

The first steps you should take are to ensure that your online footprint is limited (or even non-existent). We know that online search companies are actually data mining corporations in disguise. We also know that they have been steadily divulging your information to the federal government. Thus, the less information you give to these data mining companies, the less they will give to the NSA.

Step one should be two-fold. First, you should start using search engines like StartPage.com to perform web searches, rather than simply using companies like Google and Yahoo. Not only will this completely obliterate their ability to build a profile on you based on your searches, but it will also cover your tracks against phishers who use data mining corporation databases to build their emailing lists. Again, it's the "two birds with one stone" approach.

Next, you need to download the browser bundle called Tor, then sign up for a Hushmail.com or SilentSender.com account (the passwords, of which, will be in your wallet or purse). This will give you the means by which to surf the Web anonymously and even send certain high-sensitivity emails without worrying about them being read by unfriendly eyes. Again, keep in mind that you aren't going to want to use Tor on a regular basis, especially if you are trying to keep your account anonymous. If you view one document that has your name or address on it, then you've already given up your anonymity. Tor is for those special emails and searches that you feel are high-priority privacy concerns.

Also, even if you are having a confidential face-to-face conversation, we mentioned in chapter 19 that you should not do so unless your mobile devices are somewhere other than where the conversation is taking place. This is very important, especially because we now know that the government has the capability of listening in through the speaker on your phone.

Social networks, unfortunately, are a pretty significant part about how the U.S. government is spying on her citizenry. In fact, some would argue that the very inception of Facebook had to do with the capability of snooping into the lives of the people using it. While we are not necessarily saying that you should not use SNUs totally, we are saying that you may not want to post even somewhat controversial opinions on your profile. If you do, your profile will undoubtedly be flagged for analysis, and they will be paying special attention to you. This would defeat the purpose of changing to a privacy-minded lifestyle. Again, we aren't saying that you should remain quiet about your various opinions. However, Facebook may not be the place to bullhorn the powers-that-be. We also feel it would be a smart idea to remove all pictures of guns from your Facebook profile, as this is sure to draw unwanted attention.

It is true that most of the strategy on how to avoid government privacy intrusion has mostly to do with what you do not do, instead of proactively doing something. In fact, if you were to simply forgo using technology as a whole, then you could effectively remain 100 percent off grid. The trickiest part is the fact that this isn't really an option, if you want to live a functional life in society. This next part of chapter 21 is concerned with how to remain as anonymous as possible, while still using the conveniences of technology.

In addition, this also begins the part where living a privacy-oriented life becomes a bit pricey.

COVERING YOUR MONEY SUPPLY

Your next step may be seen as somewhat of a financial burden, but it is more like an investment.

At this point, you are going to want to start converting your digital dollars into cash and silver. Not only will this give you the ability to continue buying goods in the event that tyranny attempts to freeze your accounts, but it will also provide a hedge against inflation. In addition, the reason why we decided to wait until now to work this step into your Invisibility Objective strategy is because you should have either several lock boxes or one good safe at this point. It is not a smart idea to keep large amounts of precious metals or cash in your home, unless they are protected by a combination or a key-entry lock.

You can begin buying your silver in several different ways. One great way is through sites like eBay and Craigslist. Also, you can go to your local precious metal seller in order to avoid shipping costs. However, before you do any of this, be sure that you check the spot pricing of silver online, so that you know you are getting a good price. It is very easy to research the spot price, and some websites and apps should give you up-to-date pricing that is accurate to within ten minutes of price fluctuations.

One smart idea may be to store your silver offsite in a small, self-storage facility. The reason is that if the feds come knocking on your door to confiscate your assets, then you won't have your silver anywhere on the property. If you paid cash for a space at your local storage facility, then they would have no way to locate your assets.

It may be a good idea to insure your precious metals, but this may be rather self-defeating. In the one hand, the government would have access to that information, but at the same time, your assets would be covered if your home burnt down. One strategy may be to insure your silver, and when it looks as if the government takeover is coming, you cancel your policy. This may be a smart call, but only if you have an eye for predicting these kinds of things. It is one time where you do not want to be caught unaware and too late.

If you have the money, now would be the best time to get an offshore bank account after you've finished converting some of your assets to silver. There is safety in diversification, meaning that if one of your assets goes down, is confiscated, or is frozen, you still have the ability to turn to the other.

The first thing you should do is contact an attorney that specializes in expat services and knows how to shelter your money from prying eyes. The attorney will likely get you to set up a trust or dummy corporation in a foreign country that is not TIEA compliant. As we mentioned in chapter 18, because the host country would have no idea who controlled the corporation, there would be no possible way that the U.S. could find out. Then, you would set up your offshore bank account in the name of that corporation, meaning that you have three solid layers of protection over your money. Keep in mind, this part of the strategy could cost you in the thousands (attorney, corporation, initial deposit), which is why we feel this is one of the last protections you should put into place.

Of course, you would be able to use a debit card from this bank, which means that you can even make card transactions, and the U.S. government would have no idea whose card you were using.

However, one interesting product that you can purchase online is the no-name debit card. It essentially removes the steps in between the offshore corporation and accessing your money. Unfortunately, it would be a little bit easier to freeze the account, but it would still be very difficult to track down. In many cases the initial deposit for these cards is about $200, but the cards themselves could cost you about $600 (because the seller knows that you are not merely using the card for groceries and fast food).

However, this may be an alternative strategy to the offshore corporation, especially if you don't have the money left after your assets are converted to cash and silver.

The reason why we decided to place the issue of money near the beginning of crafting your anti-surveillance strategy is because it is important that you only use untraceable sources of funding in order to purchase the next parts of your strategy. This defeats one of the four categories of surveillance: transaction.

COVERING YOUR COMMUNICATIONS

We know that the U.S. government monitors communications. Anything said over a wire, broadcast, from a mobile device, or from a computer is instantly captured by the NSA and stored for later use or scrutiny. This is a serious privacy concern, given the fact that the majority of our communication is done through these monitored systems. Essentially, it means that the watchers have our most intimate conversations recorded and stored. But that does not have to be the case.

Your next order of business has to do with buying the prepaid phone. This shouldn't cost you more than $50 to buy minutes and the device itself (provided you buy one of the inexpensive devices). As we mentioned in chapter 19, it is important that you are not seen by CCTV cameras when purchasing this phone, and only use cash when buying it. If the watchers are attempting to locate the phone, then they will not be able to track the sale using these methods. It's important to understand the CCTV aspect of your transaction. It's through facial recognition (which is being used on current drivers licenses) that they would be able to determine your identity. This is one reason why you should try to buy the phone in either a store that does not use CCTV or attempt to subtly obstruct your facial features with a hat or sunglasses. However, if you do end up looking suspicious when purchasing the phone, you may be reported to the authorities anyway, so attempt to be as subtle as possible, while still not giving the CCTV any of your identifying features.

There are some services that can be found online that offer the ability to purchase a foreign mobile phone that uses an Asian-based chip system. While the NSA would be able to monitor the call, they would have no idea who they are listening to. In fact, you would not have to go through the rigmarole of avoiding security cameras inside the store, as many of these privacy companies buy these devices through a third-party seller. In addition, the name on the serial number would be registered to some random person in a foreign country who may not even exist. Essentially, these types of phones are seen as being totally anonymous.

However, they come with a $700 price tag, meaning that it may be smarter for you to go with the $50 option. Overall, it is best not to use your phone unless you have to, and do not keep the battery attached, as the location of the phone itself would be a dead giveaway to who owned it.

This leads us to the next purchase that you would need to make, which is that $90 signal-blocking pouch. We recommend that if you are going to keep a secondary phone, be sure to store it in one of these. Then, if you are going to use the phone, make sure that you are away from your residence. The further you are from home, the more anonymous the communication will be. Remember, they can track the phone itself; so anytime you take your phone out of the pouch ...they know where the phone (and its owner) is located. Your phone covers two of the basic tracking categories that we listed above, which is location and communication.

However, you should also put into place your methods of sending anonymous privacy-mail. Essentially, you need to craft a strategy with your recipient concerning the addresses at which you will contact him or her and the address at which they will contact you. The more mail you send from one address to another, the more you will be flagged by the watchers at the United States Postal Service.

This is important, because we mentioned before that the USPS is actively monitoring the outsides of letters and remembering the metadata. This means that every time you send a letter, they will be tracking the origination and destination of that letter. If you have 100 sets of correspondence going back and forth, and the person to whom you are sending the letter is a target, then you have also become a surveillance target.

Of course, if you have three different possible addresses between you and your recipient, then you have stretched their logistics a little bit further. It may be enough to stump them. If you keep sending the letters from false return addresses, then you've further increased their logistical load, because now they have to figure out where the letters are coming from. The only real accurate address that is necessary is the recipient's.

Unfortunately, because the United States' identity laws have become extremely tight since 9/11, you can no longer get mail drop services in America. A mail drop is basically a third-party address that you can rent temporarily without furnishing any kind of identification. However, you can still accomplish sort of the same thing, only it will cost a lot more.

On any given day, there are always classified ads for renting office space, garage space, etc. In many of these private ads, you can simply rent out these spaces with little to no identification, and some will not even run a credit check. This means that you have a totally clean address without having to provide your real name. In addition, you could also use a convincing fake ID, as most private property owners will not have access to a state identity database to confirm or deny the ID's authenticity. This way, in the event that a tyrannical government is watching mail going in and out of your address, they will have no idea that your office down the street (the one that's being rented by a Mr. John Doe), is sending an receiving the privacy-sensitive important correspondence. Perhaps the only drawback to this part of the strategy is that it could cost you hundreds per month. Again, you get what you pay for in terms of privacy protections.

One other recommendation is to only use professional courier services. However, this will cost a lot more than using the USPS. We do know that some courier services have explicit confidentiality agreements, which is a great way to go if you have something very important, but highly sensitive to send.

Also, be sure to get your hands on ultra-violet ink, which should only cost you about $2.00 per pen. This way, you can possibly avoid a sneak-and-peek attack on the content of your letter. Of course, the government says they would never do such a thing, but they haven't exactly proven themselves to be truthful on these matters.

STRATEGY ON IDENTIFICATION AND DRIVER'S LICENSES

One reason why we decided to make identification the next step in your strategy is because it often requires anonymous communication in order to get your hands on an ID that's going to be clean. Because just about everything we do is tracked in some way, it is important to have an untraceable way to conduct business, open various accounts, and even purchase vehicles and property.

Having a clean identity is perhaps one of the most difficult aspects of going off grid, as we mentioned before. However, from our perspective, you may not necessarily need to spend thousands of dollars on attorneys and a second citizenship in order to move about and conduct transactions unnoticed.

Again, this has to do with the threat versus resources balance that we've been talking about. Especially if your timing is right, you may never even have to present identification that will have the capability of passing a database check. At the same time, it is important to slowly build up your capabilities, so that if the government takeover occurs, you will have a certain level of preparedness already stored away.

One of the first things you may want to do is locate an overseas, fake ID manufacturer online. The reason why it is important to use an overseas manufacturer is because stringent U.S. laws make it illegal to sell quality, non-novelty fake identification in America. Buying overseas will ensure that the quality remains high, and they can even provide a working magnetic strip on the back. Nevertheless, in terms of strategy, it is important that you lock away this fake ID. Never use it until you absolutely have to. Attempting to use a fake ID is highly illegal.

The very reason for possessing the means by which to make your current identity disappear is not for conducting illegal activities in this era. The whole purpose is to possess the capability to avoid detainment during the possible persecution to come. This is why you should purchase your fake ID and keep it locked away in your home safe—along with the plethora of other documents that you want to keep out of sight.

Again, keep in mind that this fake identification may be able to deceive someone who simply looks at it, but it will not pass a database check. This means that, if you are stopped by the government's boots on the ground, you may be in hot water if the fake ID is what you have for identification.

However, your fake ID may be able to get you into an apartment or living space without using your real name. You should be able to acquire storage space through a private small storage unit renter, and as we said above, you might also be able to acquire office space as well. A $70 quality fake ID can essentially match the capabilities of a real one, provided it does not have to undergo a check against a database.

At the point where you possess a fake ID, it is now time to attempt to acquire a totally clean identity. This will take time, money, attorneys, and lots of effort. However, it will be worth it. Basically, you will be acquiring a totally legal, bona fide secondary driver's license from a foreign country, without having to use your actual legal name, under which you are listed as a U.S. citizen.

Some have reported that this ID does not protect them if they are driving, but others have, in fact, had success. It is for this reason that it is important to hire attorneys that specialize in this field (we recommend doing a thorough StartPage.com search), because these ordinances can change from municipality to municipality. However, what this ID will do is provide you with the capability of acquiring a place of residence, a vehicle, and even a U.S.-based bank account without ever having to put your real name on it. It is one of the best ways to deal incognito, and it still utilizes legal loopholes, meaning that you are not technically breaking the law.

The major drawback here is the fact that it may run you about $4,000 to get the foreign driver's license into your hands. This is why we feel as if it is important that you purchase the cheaper fake ID first, and then make this the next step for which you save. Also, though you may not be able to drive with it in this era, this ID is not considered fake; it may merely be invalid, in your own municipality. A fake ID under martial law would raise all kinds of red flags, but an invalid one may simply come up as a paperwork problem. Because martial law is sure to overstretch the logistical capabilities of local governments, they may simply wave you on so that they don't have to deal with the problem.

Your ability to get your hands on a clean identity will facilitate your next move to acquiring a clean place of residence. If you are, in fact, able to get a second ID, then this becomes rather simple.

WHERE SHALL WE GO?

One of the scariest parts about martial law is the fact that persecuted populations may have nowhere to go when it sets in. Simply put, the boys in black ski masks will be kicking in doors, taking names, and hauling the innocent away to re-education camps. It happened many times before in history, so there is no reason why we should not prepare for it to happen again.

Sure, you can run. You may leave as shadows before the dawn. But, where would you go? If there is a reward for turning in anyone who fits in the persecuted demographic profile, then it will be impossible to operate on a system of trust. You wouldn't be able to find a campsite, much less a piece of property. If you don't have a piece of land, a house, a closet, even a parking spot to access without giving your name (the means by which you will be tracked and pursued), then you are forced to squat —which is arguably a more dangerous scenario.

The problem with squatting (setting up a primitive form of residence that is not occupied, but still owned, by another entity) is that eventually, you will most likely be found. The variables involved with squatting may force you to pack up quickly and run every couple of days, which will adversely affect your ability to survive (much less maintain any reasonable standard or quality of life). The homeless can somewhat successfully accomplish squatting. However, that may change during martial law. Also, if you squat in communities, take over rundown properties (about which, you will likely know very little), or even live out of your car, you will have to constantly deal with the issue of crime, and you will always be concerned about being discovered by authorities.

Remember that they are looking for your demographic, and they know that they've already kicked you out of your homes and detained the ones that didn't leave. This means that they will be tracking down, rooting out, and rounding up squatters wherever they are reported, discovered, and observed.

If you do not have a clean property (a property that you legitimately own, rent, or control without the paperwork leading back to your identity) then your life will become very, very difficult when martial law is set up.

Again, this is one reason why we suggested getting your hands on a clean (or even fake) identification first, before tackling the issue of acquiring a retreat property. It is through buying property, without using your real name, that is how you will be able to effectively and safely disappear during martial law. You need a secret place to go.

However, in keeping with the threat versus resources balance, we do not recommend bankrupting yourself in an attempt to quickly buy property. This is why we are suggesting this step near the end of this chapter. We aren't saying that it is less important, but we are saying that it may not be feasible for the common person to take this step right at the beginning. There are certainly other elements of living off grid that are cheaper and easier to tackle first. Some protection is better than no protection. In addition, it does require the ability to communicate and utilize a different name in order to effectively acquire a clean place of residence. Also, rather than drawing from your own bank account to make the purchase, you should use the funds that you saved up in your offshore account or liquidate a portion of your silver. No part of this transaction should be traceable in any way.

Interestingly enough, if you were able to acquire a secondary ID, then all you really need to do is buy property through that name. Again, you will probably want to discuss these things with an attorney in order to accomplish this without raising any suspicion.

Also, purchasing this retreat property through your offshore corporation, using funds from your offshore account, would be perhaps the most untraceable method you could utilize. While this is likely to cost you considerably more, what you would get in terms of privacy would be unparalleled. Major corporations often employ these tactics for the purpose of tax avoidance and hiding their plans from the public eye. However, this will mean that you need to hire an attorney and be able to fund the operation, which could cost quite a lot.

You might also decide to purchase property through a land trust. The downside of that is, the information for who controls the property would be located in the U.S. Remember, martial law does not subscribe to constitutional law. If your property raises any flags, they will eventually find out who is on the paperwork. In addition, if the U.S. ever makes it worthwhile for your attorney to divulge your information, then this may be a bad situation for you. Also, your attorney would technically control the property. Either way, it is still an option, as your name is not technically connected with the ownership of the property.

Of course, the above options can cost you quite a bit. If your funds are limited, you may not have the capability to purchase property through legal loopholes. If this is the case, one way you might be able to acquire a place of residence is through networking. For instance, you may not always have to produce identification in order to rent an apartment. Sometimes private landlords do not go through the formality of credit and identity checks, meaning that you maybe able to acquire the space in a different name (or be listed there under the landlord's name).

However, if this is something that you do, make sure that you aren't paying rent, utilities, and other services in your name or directly from your own bank account. This is an obvious giveaway, simply because they will track your bank account transactions to the address listed on the bills. You should only pay through cash, money orders, or even checks from your offshore account. This may take some negotiation, and it may not be the easiest set-up to find, but you will have a place to go when martial law is instated.

Overall, it is important that you only go through people you can trust when purchasing or renting property. Never mention your address or the existence of this property to anyone outside your closest circle. Anytime you have to write down the address, make sure that you are doing so through untraceable means that can't track back to you.

In addition, never take your own mobile phone to or access wireless Internet from this apartment. You may use your secondary phone or computer at this apartment, but only do so in a limited way so that you do not accidentally betray your protections.

TRANSPORTATION

Last, purchase your vehicle through your new identity (or in the name of your dummy corporation) and address, paying for it in cash. Registering this vehicle in your secondary identity will be completely and totally legal. In addition, this will further cement your new identity with the state, as this is one of the first aspects of an identity that is checked. If your vehicle is run through a database, it will show up as legal and in your secondary name, which will be seen as validation of your legitimacy. However, you should never drive this vehicle with your own identification, as you should only do so with your foreign driver's license. Also, be sure to purchase car insurance through your secondary identity in order to ensure that, if you are pulled over while driving it, there are no red flags that pop up. In addition, your own phone should never be caught in the same location as your off-grid vehicle.

Because you have put all of your identity building blocks in place, you can actually purchase insurance using the same methods we've been describing above. Every purchase you make for your anti-surveillance/martial law protection can flow through this new entity that you have created.

IN REVIEW

Overall, it is important that you start with the beginning steps and then build your way up. Like building blocks, you need to re-create yourself apart from your own identity. This is likely going to cost you a fair amount of money, but there are certain levels of protection that you can put in place that will not break the bank. Here is a chronological list, a theoretical guide and blueprint if you will, of how best to begin:

1. Use untraceable methods of online research
2. Move to untraceable means of email
3. Clean up social networking profiles
4. Purchase safe
5. Begin saving cash and silver
6. Purchase mobile device signal-blocking case
7. Purchase prepaid mobile phone with cash—immediately place phone in signal-blocking case

8. Find trustworthy (personally known, if possible) attorney who specializes in expat/tax avoidance law

9. Through attorney, use cash saved to purchase and set up offshore corporation and corresponding bank account

10. Set up no-name bank card, separate from offshore account

11. Purchase fake ID through untraceable means—use courier service (not USPS)

12. For mail correspondence, rent temporary office space through fake ID

13. Acquire official foreign ID through temporary office space correspondence

14. Acquire Asia-based, chipped anonymous phone through temporary office space correspondence—immediately place phone in signal-blocking case with other mobile phone

15. Purchase property through offshore corporation

16. Close down temporary office, move office address to property

17. Purchase vehicle through new address, bank account, and foreign ID— keep on property

By the time you reach number sixteen, these protections should merely sit dormant until they are needed. This entire chapter is nothing more than a grand Stage Three in the Invisibility Objective, as they should not be put into use until martial law is finally declared.

As time marches on, you should slowly acquire supplies, food, and other items that make life possible, storing all of it on your new property. There should not be one receipt, transaction, serial number, or photo that links your birth identity and your secondary one. This means that any purchase that makes it to your property should be acquired only through your secondary identity. Never bring a GPS, mobile device, or your own vehicle to this new property.

Essentially, you should become a new person entirely. The person you were at birth should not be the person you are when supplying, utilizing, or running as your secondary identity. The one should not even have the possibility of appearing to know the other, except perhaps, only through the same attorney's office that you happen to have in common.

Chapter 22

NOT PRIVACY—DIGNITY

In this book, we have certainly covered quite a few horrifying scenarios. Between identity thieves who can hack into your smartphone, corporations who can see when you open your fridge, and government who is collecting your text messages, it may feel as if there is just nowhere to go anymore. When not even your home is private, one must wonder if the last privacy we have left is our thoughts. Even then, perhaps they want to know our minds as well.

The desire for privacy and personal space is not one of criminality—it is of humanity. The need to keep certain parts of our lives to ourselves is integrally important to the health of our souls. It is a need that is rooted so deeply into our core that the denial of this need feels like a violation of the soul. Understanding the depth of this need is why governments use the denial of privacy as punishment for crime in the form of constant surveillance in tightly packed, humiliating prisons.

When understanding how extensively our society is surveilled, it can feel as if we are being punished for our freedoms in the grand prison of the police state. The feeling that there is no escape is maddening. With every new story about government surveillance programs, the walls close in a little bit closer, and we are left with less and less of the substance of our own dignified humanity.

Then, perhaps that is it. Perhaps, this has less to do with privacy…and more to do with dignity.

With every wiretap, hack, and extraction of metadata, our dignity slips away through our American fingers, fingers that once gripped so tightly to it mere decades ago. Privacy is the tool that facilitates our dignity.

Every time the U.S. government chips away at our privacy, peering into the most intimate parts of our lives and lie, saying that, "It is for your own good," they dissolve the dignity of the citizens who keep them in power. When the government shows their mistrust in their own populace, treading upon the laws that the American people once codified, and openly violates decency itself, they chisel the foundations of our dignity. And, they wonder why the citizenry is angry?

We pay our taxes; we keep the laws; we vote them into office; we fight their wars; we cheer for them; we honor them; and we give of our emotions, thoughts, and energies to see this nation thrive. Yet, they feel the need to insult us by treating law-abiding Americans like naughty children. Then, when one citizen does tell the truth, that individual is ridiculed, demonized, and sent running for his life, never to see his native land for the rest of his days. It is no wonder Americans of all walks of life, ethnicities, creeds, and philosophies are becoming disgusted and apathetic. There is now a growing resentment and mistrust from the populace, much like the kind we have been shown.

When we read, to our horror, that bureaucracies are buying ammunition, when drones fill our skies, and our emails are not considered by government to be private correspondence, what exactly are we to think? The federal government is constantly moving towards aggression, not against foreign-based enemies, but against the good people of this nation. Why? What is their reason? We are not militarily organizing against them, but they are organizing their forces against us.

This does not appear to be done for our protection. Instead, it smacks of domestic invasion. The general sends his spies before the army, so perhaps we should be expecting the army soon. Unfortunately, it seems to have come to this.

THE PHILOSOPHY OF THE INVISIBILITY OBJECTIVE

The Invisibility Objective has nothing to do with breaking laws, and it has nothing to do with being sneaky per se. The whole point of the Invisibility Objective is to keep our dignity in an undignified world. It is to prepare for the consequences of a society that forgets the importance of strong laws that protect them from the government. Our society seems to have neglected to remember the words of President George Washington:

Government is not reason; it is not eloquent; it is force. Like fire, it is a dangerous servant and a fearful master.

Understanding this, it seems rather appropriate to regard the government as a fire. Americans have forgotten that this fire, which is certainly helpful to us, is dangerous. Well, that fire has now spread from its rightful place and has begun consuming our homes.

The Invisibility Objective is not concerned with throwing water on the fire (as we believe that time may have passed). Our concern is with getting out of the house before it burns to the ground.

Of course, it is always possible to wildly run out of the house without our shoes, a bag packed, and a change of clothes, but then life simply goes from bad to worse. No, our approach is concerned with exiting the house in a safe, organized manner, having a safe place afterwards to lay our heads at night, and being able to get on with the more important parts of our lives. We do not fear the fire, but we respect its uncontrolled ability to destroy.

As the temperature rises and the smoke begins to billow in our home, we begin to pack. Because we do not know when the fire will cut off our escape to freedom, we may need to pack quickly. However, the fact that we are aware of the danger and are sensitive to the heat and smoke means that we do not have to pack frantically. The Invisibility Objective is about preparing to leave in a methodical way, taking care to ensure that we are not trapped inside a burning building, and escaping in a way that allows us to leave in a dignified manner.

THE IDENTITY GAME

Where the metaphor of the fire falls short is the fact that the government is less predictable, harder to control, and it seems to have malicious intent. This is the only fire that wants to burn you.

For this reason, we must also respect, not fear, the issue of human nature. Where there is power, there will be corruption. At the end of the day, everybody wants to get paid, and everybody wants to keep a desk. The folks in the government are no different than the rest of us.

This is why we must learn to leave behind our former identities when the fire tries to cut off our escape. The hard part of disappearing is not the act itself. It is continuing life in the state of disappearance. This is where most folks attempting to hide will get burned in the end.

In addition, the mistakes we may likely commit will not have occurred after we run, but while we were packing our bags. This is why we stress the understanding that you must be methodical, logical, and thorough when transitioning from one entity to the next. One accidental login from your own computer, one time taking a call at your retreat, one transaction from your own bank account, and your entire effort to evade the eyes of martial law could be stopped by a hard knock at the door, followed by a flash-bang grenade.

The preparations you take after reading this book may also be seen as deviant, unacceptable, and even illegal. Though these preparations are none of the three, it is important that you value this fact. Folks who find something offensive tend to talk about it. Of course, it may make you feel better by telling naysayers a thing or two, but it will certainly not help forward your objective. You should never talk about your preparations with anyone (except perhaps your spouse or closest confidant), and you should always respect the awful power of gossip.

The way you must set up your second identity is to ensure that your first stays as far away from your second as possible. Nothing, absolutely no paperwork, communication, location, or transaction should lead back to the person you are today. The origin of person number two must be an enigma, and the disappearance of person number one must be mystery. And as we said in the last chapter, the only common relation between person-one and person-two is the fact that these persons just so happened to use the same attorney at one time. It is this attention to detail that will save you in the end, clear your name, and allow you to live somewhat freely. Your second identity could never have committed one of their crimes, held a controversial opinion, or even been a part of a persecuted demographic because…well…this person has been the model citizen with no questionable associations and a social footprint smaller than an infant's.

IDENTITY THEFT FACTOR

While identity theft appears to be a totally separate issue from government privacy intrusion, the two are very much the same in the idea that both completely ignore the inherent dignity of the victim.

However, it is important to look at the two through the eyes of statistical possibility. Perhaps one reason why many fear government privacy intrusion more than identity theft is because if martial law occurs, it will affect everyone. On the flip side of that coin, the reason why many fear identity theft more than government privacy intrusion is because identity theft is already occurring, and it might affect us. Either way, there is a chance that both will happen to us in our lifetimes, and that chance is increasing with every advance in technology's influence in our lives.

Nevertheless, identity theft is like any other crime: it is the violation of laws that protect private property. This means, in order to guard yourself against it, you must prepare in advance, foil the crime while it is being perpetrated, or catch the criminal(s) after the fact. Essentially, these are the three stages of the Invisibility Objective. In a way, the Invisibility Objective can be applied to just about any crime.

One reason why we continually arrive at the notion of applying statistics to the possibility of identity theft in your life is because it is the application of the Invisibility Objective that will lower your chances of being affected. Unfortunately, you must live on an island and never interact with anything human to bring those chances down to zero. The entire purpose of the Invisibility Objective, when applied to identity theft, is to manage your chances of being attacked and increase the risk of the attacker. When this happens, you will notice that peace of mind will follow.

In fact, much of the need to protect yourself from identity theft from occurring in your life has much to do with your peace of mind. Frankly, the most devastating effect of identity theft has to do with the fear and paranoia that the victim experiences and less to do with the actual financial damage involved. Statistically speaking, identity theft usually doesn't inflict a hefty amount of damage in a monetary sense, but an individual can be emotionally scarred for years thereafter.

This is why it is important to understand that the real objective in this book, the purpose for which it was written, is not necessarily one that merely looks at the bottom line. Instead, our purpose was to provide you with the tools to achieve peace of mind through introducing the facts and not entertaining you with trinkets and psychobabble.

CONCLUSION

In *Underground Privacy Secrets,* we have spent much of our time exploring the different aspects of privacy protection. Whether from government, corporations, or private criminals, we hope that you were able to learn how to defend yourself from folks who would use your good name for their purposes without your consent.

In this book, our defenses were less concerned with an active system, but rather a passive one that is dependent on stealth, evasion, and strategy. For the common person, secrecy and deception work the best, as it requires fewer resources in order to stave off disaster, while avoiding a risky standoff. For instance, flaunting an unbreakable safe is a great way to attract thieves who are up to the task. Yes, you may foil a hundred, but it only takes one. In addition, the Invisibility Objective can work extremely well for the simple fact that our enormous numbers work in our favor.

With more than 300 million documented Americans in the U.S., the logistical load for government surveillance systems is tremendous. This is one reason why they are spending massive amounts of resources for their technology to catch up with the logistical demand. In the same way, those hundreds of millions of Americans are also potential targets for identity theft. This means that if you remain difficult to notice, then identity thieves will simply move to a different target. They will not go out of their way to hit what they cannot see.

One of these lessons we've learned is the importance of strong property and privacy laws. It is these laws that protect the common person from both identity theft and government privacy intrusion. Strong property laws not only preserve freedom, but they also provide an excellent deterrent against identity theft. The opposite of this is in third-world countries, where often the laws exist, but enforcement of them is lacking. This creates a breeding ground for sophisticated identity theft operations, affecting individuals in countries thousands of miles away.

Of course, it is not really the government's concern to protect every single American from identity theft. In fact, it is mostly up to the individual to ensure that his or her privacy and identity remain protected. Ultimately, it is through common sense practices and basic knowledge of your home network that is the best deterrent against identity theft.

In the same way, it is also up to each citizen to hold the government's feet to the fire, staying informed about the steps they're taking against individual privacy. Where this fails is when the government has finally gone out of control: even when they get caught, they simply continue without batting an eye. This is beginning to happen now.

This is why ensuring that data mining corporations and government collect as little information on us as possible is crucial. Like any entity, the more information it collects, the more powerful and dangerous it can become.

Empowering yourself to care for your own identity is one of the hallmarks of a responsible person. Doing the same to care for your own privacy is one of the hallmarks of a responsible citizen. This kind of vigilant responsibility is hard to victimize, since it is strategic, logical, and methodic in nature. In addition, a truly responsible citizenry has always carried the moral high ground and the law on their side.

The Constitution grants us liberty. It is up to us to preserve our own privacy and uphold the rule of law.